THE ARMY CHAPLAIN

His Office, Duties, and Responsibilities,

AND THE

MEANS OF AIDING HIM.

THE REV. W. Y. BROWN, A.M.,

HOSPITAL CHAPLAIN, UNITED STATES ARMY.

Reprinted from the 1863 edition by W.Y. Brown. and published by William S. and Alfred Martien, Philadelphia, Pennsylvania. Original spellings and format have been preserved where possible.

This edition copyright © 2010 Sparklight Press.

Cover photograph: Chaplain conducting mass for the 69th New York State Militia encamped at Fort Corcoran, Washington, D.C., 1861. Photographed by Matthew B. Brady. National Archives, Washington, D.C.

ISBN 978-1-934788-00-4

Library of Congress Subject Heading: United States. Army—Chaplains.

Published in the United States by
    Sparklight Press
    Tyler, Texas
    sparklightpress.com

10 9 8 7 6 5 4 3

PREFACE.

As the duties of the Chaplain in the army are very imperfectly defined, it has occurred to the writer, that a small work upon the subject was needed, and would add to the efficiency of the corps, and be of service to the army and the country.

Desiring to bring the work within the requirements of the Army Regulations, he has omitted several topics, which he would otherwise have discussed, which lie beyond the range of existing laws and regulations.

It is also hoped that a more definite knowledge, by the immediate friends and relatives of the soldiers, of the character and extent of the religious privileges to which they are entitled in the field and the hospital, will lessen their anxieties, and in some measure, mitigate their sufferings on their behalf.

W. Y. B.

DOUGLAS HOSPITAL, WASHINGTON, D. C.

April 24, 1863.

CONTENTS.

INTRODUCTION.
FITNESS FOR THE DUTIES OF THE OFFICE OF CHAPLAIN.

A difficult field of labor. — Piety, the highest qualification. — Must be "apt to teach." — A lively temperament and obliging disposition, requisite. — Of resolute purpose. — Energy of character. — Vigorous health and strong constitution. — Self-possession. — Self-control.

17-22

PART I.

THE HOSPITAL CHAPLAIN.

CHAPTER I.
APPOINTMENT.

The President's Message. — Original appointees. — The origin of the office. — One to each permanent Hospital.

— How appointed. — Legal qualifications. — Certificate of appointment. — Assimulated rank. — Surgeon, the commanding officer. — Duties distinct. — The Uniform—when to be worn. — Reasons for. — Compensation. — Quarters should be convenient. — Assigned to duty. — Leave of absence.

23-31

Chapter II.

The Chapel and Its Services.

Chapel necessary. — Reasonable facilities allowed. — Ward not adapted to chapel service. — Dining-room inconvenient. — Preaching in the chapel. — Preparation for. — Audience peculiar. — Officers part of. — Educated men in the ranks. — Convalescent soldiers. — Gratitude. — Inquiring; despondency. — Spiritual murder. — Short services. — Themes. — Denominationalism eschewed. — Evening prayers; family worship. — What exercises. — Weekly lecture. — Importance of.

33-40

Chapter III.

The Chaplain in the Ward.

Delicate duties. — Backslider reclaimed. — The careless and unawakened sinner. — Difficulties; dangers. — The last hour! — Importance of. — The Christian hero. — Happy experience. — A quiet ward, the contrary. —

Cheerfulness. — Tenderness. — Daily fruits. — Prayer in the ward; public, private. — Prayer suggested.

41-45

Chapter IV.

Letter-Writing.

Great influx of patients. — Anxieties of friends. — Mails inaccessible. — Friends relieved; patient benefitted. — Battles, exaggerated rumors of. — Stationery obtained. — Postage; letters franked. — Patients who cannot write. — Chaplains' letters. — Assistants. — Patients hesitate. — False view. — Harassing situation. — False system of morality. — Truth is purity. Truthfulness enjoined.

47-50

Chapter V.

Treatment of Cases of Special Religious Interest.

Sanctified afflictions. — Inquirers. — Careful treatment of. — Difficult task. — Difficulties to be ascertained. — Anxieties of the physician. — Soul more important than the body. — Necessity of notes. — Importance of notes of special cases. — Surgeon's notes published. — The desponding. — Diagnosis of the case. — Characteristics of the despondency of the true believer; of the nominal Christian. — Cause and effect. — Nervous debility. — God's sovereignty. — Unfaithfulness. — The

Skeptic. — Infidelity, negative. — Controversy eschewed. — Reason of the hope that is in him, given. — Christ offered.

51-58

CHAPTER VI.

THE DYING; THE DEAD AND THEIR BURIAL.

Dying among strangers. — Interrogatories of friends. — His feelings and prospects ascertained. — The parting word. — Facts communicated to nearest kin. — Important letters. — Chaplain's Register—Form—Necessity of. — Clerical assistance. — Soldiers' identity. — Religious belief. — Burial of the dead. — Grave among strangers. — Burial service. — The hour fixed. — Escort.

59-66

CHAPTER VII.

GAMES—READING MATTER.

Mind is active. — Scientific games. — Games of chance. — Petty gambling. — Cards forbidden. — Reading matter; religious, secular. — Books labeled,—Librarian. — The Scriptures in the wards. — Tracts and religious newspaper. — How furnished. — Reading-room and daily papers.

67-71

CHAPTER VIII.

DISCIPLINE.

Hospital rules and regulations. — Discipline expected and necessary. — Sabbath observance, President's order, Army regulations concerning. — Profanity. — Drunkenness. — Moral sense. — Hospital discipline, theoretically and practically. — Local vices. — Judicious suggestions.

73-77

CHAPTER IX.

MATTERS FOREIGN TO

THE OFFICE OF THE CHAPLAIN.

Numberless matters pressed upon him. — A good rule. — Exceptions. — Men confide in him. — Inquiries and complaints. — Abuses corrected. — Harmony of feeling between chaplain and surgeon.

79-81

PART II.

REGIMENTAL AND POST CHAPLAIN.

CHAPTER I.
REGIMENTAL CHAPLAIN, APPOINTMENT.

Number allowed. — How appointed. — Legal qualifications. — Compensation. — Mustered into the service. — Staff officer. — Manner of appointing not uniform. — Practice of the several States. — Is he a commissioned officer? — Grave questions involved. — The uniform. — Duties not defined. — Moral courage. — Position created. — Attaché.

85-91

CHAPTER II.
PUBLIC RELIGIOUS INSTRUCTION.

A pastoral charge. — Spurs to diligence. — Perils of professors of religion. — Family restraints wanting. — Wicked associations. — The unregenerate. — Fearful condition. — Important provision. — Sabbath service. — The church-call. — Slight excuse. — Weekly prayer-meeting and lecture. — Prayer at dress parade. — The mess; family prayers. — Family worship in the parish. — The tent; a pleasant hour.

93-98

Chapter III.

Pastoral Visitation.

The social principle. — Acquaintanceship. — Moral status ascertained. — Personal intercourse. — Private Register. — Prudence and discretion. — Regularity tends to efficiency. — A wily enemy dislodged. — Casual circumstances improved. — God's agencies. — Unwarned. — The blood of souls!

99-103

Chapter IV.

The Sick and Wounded in the Camp.

Regimental and division hospital. — The chaplain welcomed. — An attractive field. — The chaplain during battle. — Appropriate duties. — The dying. — General hospital.

105-107

Chapter V.

Religious Reading.

Religious press. — Newspapers. — Communication with publication houses. — A missing link; what is it? — The best of all reading. — A convenient book. — Shirt pocket. — Power of divine truth. — The fly-leaf made useful. — "Unknown," a melancholy inscription.

109-112

CHAPTER VI.
QUARTERLY REPORT. CAMP VICES.

Legal requirements. — Information needed and given. — Morality essential to discipline. — Official suggestions to commanding officer. — Careful preparation needed. — Important files. — Camp vices. — Immorality denounced. — Important command. — Baptism of tears. — Defective systems of morals. — The source of permanent reformation.

113-117

CHAPTER VII.
THE POST-CHAPLAIN.

Number of. — Appointment of. — To reside at post. — Compensation. — A chapel necessary. — Public services, kind and extent. — Bible Class. — Library of bound books. — Librarian. — Other religious reading. — The school-master. — Who have a right to instruction? — Assistants. — Responsibility. — What is expected?

119-123

PART III.

AID TO THE CHAPLAIN.

The highest good to the soldier—The word of God. — The American Bible Society. — Religious books. —

Demand greater than the supply. — Boards of Publication. — Religious Newspapers. — The Christian Commission's Appeal. — Profitable reading. — An unending wave. — Two great agencies: the Sanitary Commission; its work and fruits. — The Christian Commission. — Its jewels. — Its aid to the chaplain. — Letters from friends, their character and usefulness. — Prayer, its importance. — Christian effort for the army, a political necessity. — Influence of returning soldiers. — The chaplaincy the great instrument. — Its defects remedied. — It must be sustained.

127-140

INTRODUCTION.

FITNESS FOR THE DUTIES OF THE OFFICE OF CHAPLAIN.

A very brief experience in the chaplaincy will be sufficient to impress any one with an abiding sense of the difficulties, responsibilities, and vastness of this field of labor; and to wring from every honest heart, the inquiry of the apostle, "Who is sufficient for these things?"

As in the Christian ministry, in general, so in this particular department of ministerial labor, the highest qualification, and without which all other qualifications avail nothing, is ardent piety. The Christian ministry is the most holy and honorable office on earth, and God has committed the exercise of its functions to pure minded, conscientious, and pious men; and whoever attempts to discharge the duties of the ministry as pertaining to the chaplain, without piety, will not only utterly fail in his efforts, but he will do incalculable mischief. He belies the nature of Christianity, and dishonors his high office. Christianity claims to be a divine institution. She professes to change the heart; to infuse a new principle of life; to exalt and beautify the external conduct, by giving to the soul pure and correct principles of action. She professes to mould, by her sanctifying influences, "a peculiar people, zealous of good works;" to write living epistles, which may be "read and known of all men;" in a word, this is Christianity—"to love the Lord our God with all our heart, with all our soul, with all our strength, and with all our mind, and our neighbor as ourselves." It is so claimed by Christ; it is so experienced by the devout; it is so acknowledged by the world; and the chaplain, in common with all other ministers, is expected to exhibit these characteristics in their greatest fulness and beauty; and wherever he is found without them, or any evidence of true piety, he sours the hearts of the men; he germinates the seeds of infidelity; and, he degrades, not only the office of the chaplain, but of the Christian ministry, and brings both into contempt in the eyes of the world.

The chaplain must be "apt to teach." Teaching is the highest duty of his office, and surely, therefore, he should be well qualified to give instruction, before assuming the responsibilities of the office. His own mind must be thoroughly stored with the great doctrines of the Bible, and all other knowledge necessary for the proper elucidation of his subject, as he cannot command that time in the camp and hospital for preparation, which might be convenient in the parish or congregation; and he is compelled to rely much more upon his own resources, and his previous mental stores, for the instruction of those under his care, than in an ordinary pastoral charge. He must often communicate instruction, too, under many unfavorable circumstances, which will tax the resources of the most gifted mind, and the most fluent speaker. Whoever has found himself deficient in this qualification, after a fair trial in the parish, need not seek the office of the chaplain with a view of increasing his usefulness: his defects will only be the more glaring, and his failure, the more signal.

A lively temperament, and a kind and obliging disposition, are also requisite. Both in the camp and in the hospital, men need to be encouraged, to be cheered up in their labors and sufferings, and it is very desirable that the very countenance, as well as the manner of the chaplain, should indicate cheerfulness; its power is magical, and irresistible among the men. Without a genial temperament, he will often find his own comfort, as well as that of the men, sadly, and perhaps often, almost unaccountably destroyed. However perplexing and harassing his situation, he must ever bear in mind that he is a Christian gentleman, which is the highest type of man, and excludes every act of rudeness, unkindness, and moroseness.

He must be a man of resolute purpose. Obstacles are constantly thrown in his pathway, which must be removed; difficulties are met, which must be overcome; and so multiplied are these, that no one, but a man of resolution, can successfully encounter them. And even he can only be properly sustained by an humble and confiding faith in the truthfulness and veracity of God, the genuineness of his promises, and in his willingness to direct, and his power to defend. In the exercise of the most dauntless courage, he must still feel that his "sufficiency is of God," and that he "can do all things through Christ which strengtheneth" him.

With resolution, he must combine energy of character, and a willing heart. A lazy chaplain is certainly an object of commiseration. While he dozes through the camp or the hospital, souls are awaking in hell, whose blood is upon his soul, and which will be required of him in the day of judgment. He is loathed by the men; despised by the officers; and ekes out his miserable existence amidst the frowns of all honest men, and the contempt of the world.

He must be a man of vigorous health and of a good constitution. In the hospital, he is constantly inhaling the atmosphere of the sick chamber, and which is frequently impregnated with contagious diseases, and if his own constitution and health are not good, his life will be in constant jeopardy. The duties, too, are so arduous, and so varied, that a man with a weak constitution or, in infirm health, is almost certain to utterly break down in discharge of the duties of the office, and to yield his life as the penalty for undertaking them.

In camp, he is constantly exposed to such extremes of weather, heat and cold, and wet and dry, and to such irregularities in living, as will often wreck the strongest constitutions, and break down the most vigorous health; and with all these facts before him, no one should seek the office who has not the physical ability to meet its requirements, and to perform its appropriate duties.

He should be a man of great self-possession. All men in the army should cultivate this excellent quality of a good soldier; and the chaplain is often placed in circumstances which require the utmost self-possession for the proper discharge of the duties of his office; and where this quality is lacking, he will be utterly helpless. There are sometimes scenes of suffering so terrible, scenes of excitement so intense, and scenes of carnage so awful, with which the chaplain comes in contact, as to completely unnerve many men, but which demand the most prompt attention and the most vigorous treatment; and sadly deficient is that chaplain, who cannot command himself at such a time, and under such circumstances.

He must be a man of general self-control. The tendency of war is to demoralization, and he must stem this tide in his own breast, as well as endeavor to resist its influence upon others. But few classes of ministers are so constantly exposed to coldness and formality and the neglect of the cultivation of personal holiness, and to vices and crimes of a deeper hue, as the chaplain; and therefore, he must be constantly on his guard, and be able to command himself, and to resist all species of temptation. This can be done by the assistance of divine grace, and by that, alone. Good men are often permitted to do many sinful things, and to wound the cause of Christ for a season; and their deep sorrow, and scalding tears of repentance, should warn every one to take heed "lest he fall."

PART I.

THE HOSPITAL CHAPLAIN.

CHAPTER I.

APPOINTMENT.

IN his message to Congress, at the commencement of the second session of the Thirty-seventh Congress, President Lincoln says: "By mere omission, I presume, Congress has failed to provide chaplains for hospitals occupied by volunteers. This subject was brought to my notice, and I was induced to draw up the form of a letter, one copy of which, properly addressed, has been delivered to each of the persons, and at the dates respectively named and stated in a schedule, containing also the form of the letter, marked A,[*] and herewith transmitted.

---

[*] Schedule A.

EXECUTIVE MANSION,
Washington, D. C., 1861.

REV. ———:

 Sir—Having been solicited by Christian ministers, and other pious people, to appoint suitable persons to act as chaplains at the hospitals for our sick and wounded soldiers, and feeling the intrinsic propriety of having such persons to so act, and yet believing there is no law conferring the power upon me to

"These gentlemen, I understand, entered upon the duties designated, at the times respectively stated in the schedule, and have labored faithfully therein ever since. I therefore recommend that they be compensated at the same rate as chaplains in the army. I further suggest that general provision be made for chaplains to serve at hospitals, as well as with regiments."

This is the origin of the hospital chaplain in the army of the United States; and exhibits, at once, the President's sympthy for the sick and wounded soldier, and his appreciation of the office of the Christian minister, to mitigate his sufferings.

Congress adopted the suggestion of the President, and provided for the appointment of a chaplain at each of the permanent hospitals in the army.[*]

---

appoint them, I think fit to say, that if you will voluntarily enter upon and perform the appropriate duties of such position, I will recommend that Congress make compensation therefor at the same rate that chaplains in the army are compensated.

The following are the names and dates respectively of the persons and times to whom and when such letters were delivered:

      Rev. G. G. Goss, September 25, 1861.
      Rev. John G. Butler, September 25, 1861.
      Rev. Henry Hopkins, September 25, 1861.
      Rev. F. M. Magrath, October 30, 1861.
      Rev. F. E. Boyle, October 30, 1861.
      Rev. John C. Smith, November 7, 1861.
      Rev. Wm. Y. Brown, November 7, 1861.

[*] Act May 20, 1862, § 2.

The hospital chaplain is appointed by the President of the United States, by and with the advice and consent of the Senate.† He must be a regularly ordained minister of some religious denomination; and he must present "testimonials of his present good standing as such minister, together with a recommendation for his appointment as an army chaplain, from some authorized ecclesiastical body, or not less than five accredited ministers belonging to said religious denomination."‡

He receives a certificate of appointment from the War Department in the form of a commission, as follows:

[Form of Commission—Hospital Chaplain.]
WAR DEPARTMENT,
Washington City, D. C., 1862.
To all who shall see these presents, greeting:
KNOW YE, That . . . . . , of . . . . . , has been, and is hereby appointed CHAPLAIN OF THE UNITED STATES HOSPITAL at . . . . . , with authority to do and discharge the duties of that office during the pleasure of the President of the United States for the time being.

Given under my hand, at the City of Washington, this . . day of . , in the year of our Lord one thousand eight hundred and sixty , and in the eighty . . year of the Independence of the United States.

By the President, ———
———, Secretary of War.

---

† Act July 17, 1862, § 9.
‡ Act July 17, 1862, § 9.

It will be observed that the certificate does not specify any definite rank. But originally having the pay of captain of cavalry, he is generally considered as having the assimulated rank of a staff captain. But the office of chaplain is one of ministry, and not of command, except in his own department of labor, and so far as may be necessary to direct subordinates in the discharge of his official duties.

The surgeon in charge is the commanding officer of the hospital, and must be obeyed, as such, by all connected with the hospital; and yet, he cannot interfere with the chaplain in his appropriate work. In the performance of his legitimate duties, the chaplain is left free and unrestrained.

But the duties of the surgeon and the chaplain are so distinct, and their interests so united, that there never can be any real conflict between them. The one pertains to the cure of the diseases of the body; the other, of the soul: both having reference to the best interests of the patient. Both desire the well-being of the men, and are equally interested in enhancing the reputation of the hospital with which they both stand connected. And while it is the privilege, as well as the duty of the chaplain, to confer with the surgeon in charge, in regard to such police regulations as affect the moral and religious interests of the patients, yet the law leaves the making, altering, and enforcing of said regulations in the hands of the surgeon in charge, and they cannot be interfered with by the chaplain.

In view of his high office as a minister of the gospel, and his position in the army, the chaplain is entitled to be treated with due respect by all officers of the hospital; and from enlisted men, he must be treated with that high respect which must ever be shown to all officers in the army.

"The uniform for chaplains of the army," says a general order of the Adjutant-General,[*] "will be, plain black frock coat, with standing collar, and one row of nine black buttons; plain black pantaloons; black felt hat or army forage cap, without ornament. On occasions of ceremony, a plain *chapeau de bras* may be worn."

This uniform is disliked by many, and is considered unmilitary by others; yet it is the prescribed uniform of the corps, and should always be worn by the chaplain when in the discharge of the duties of his office. "Officers at their stations, in camp or in garrison, will always wear their proper uniform," is the language of the Army Regulations,[*] and the requirement is as binding upon the chaplain as any other officer in the army. And independently of the requirements of the Regulations, there is a peculiar and urgent necessity for the hospital chaplain to be in uniform always when on duty. New patients are

---

[*] No. 102. 1861.
[*] § 114.

constantly arriving, and being mingled with others in the several wards, and some of them may desire, and may need, the immediate attention of the chaplain; and every one should be able to recognise this officer the moment he enters the ward, and be able to distinguish him from the surgeon on the one hand, and from civilians and visitors upon the other.

In large military hospitals, the chaplain cannot converse with each patient every day, and it might not be desirable if he could; but he should visit each ward every day, and thus give an opportunity for any who may desire to speak with him, to do so; and unless he is in uniform, and easily recognised as such officer, this opportunity will not be afforded to the men. There is a natural distrust of strangers among soldiers, and at the same time a strong sympathy and community of feeling in the army among the officers and the men; and the moment the chaplain, in his proper uniform, approaches the bedside of a soldier, he is immediately recognised as a fellow-soldier, a sympathizing friend, and the patient's heart is at once open to such instruction as he may see fit to communicate.

The compensation of the chaplain is one hundred dollars per month, and two rations when on duty, and forage in kind for one horse.

Where his quarters are not in the hospital, they should be so convenient to it as to be easily accessible at all hours when he is at them, so that he may be called in a moment. It is his duty to visit the bedside of the sick and dying soldier at any hour that he may desire the services of the chaplain, and give such counsel and advice as the case may demand, and to afford such consolation to the dying as our holy religion is calculated to afford in this solemn hour. This may often occur at night, and when an hour may be eternity to the soul, and must not be consumed in sending to a distance for him.

Hospital chaplains are assigned by the Surgeon-General to hospitals in the cities for which they have been appointed; and all chaplains are subject to such rules, in relation to leave of absence from duty, as are prescribed for other officers at such posts.[*]

---

[*] General Order No. 78. 1862.

CHAPTER II.

THE CHAPEL, AND ITS SERVICES.

IN every military hospital, a suitable room should always be reserved, to be used exclusively as a chapel; and it should be appropriately furnished for such use. In the exigencies of an active campaign, hospitals may be extemporized in churches and other buildings, where it may be impracticable to furnish a suitable room for a chapel; and it may be necessary to conduct the religious services in the wards or dining-room; but these are extreme cases, and should be the exception.

No buildings should be hired or built by the Government for a general hospital, without making appropriate provision for a chapel. In creating the office, Congress evidently designed that the chaplain should have every reasonable facility for the discharge of the appropriate duties of his office; and the public preaching of the gospel, is the highest duty and privilege of the Christian minister. Whether as a minister or a chaplain, he possesses, ordinarily, no other means of usefulness, comparable to the oral preaching of the gospel. God has established the ministry preeminently for this purpose. It is his plan of unfolding the great doctrines of salvation to sinners, and of winning souls to Christ. Other means and agencies are important, and have their appropriate place, but in the congregation, and among the convalescents in the hospital, these are all subordinate to the public oral promulgation of the gospel.

This cannot be done in the ward where there are very sick men; and where they are convalescent, but few more than the usual occupants of the ward, can be admitted. The dining-room cannot be readily prepared for the services, and it is generally unsuited for the purpose, if it could; and it would be altogether impracticable to use it as often as religious services in the chapel are desirable. Besides, the room which is specifically and exclusively devoted to religious services, becomes at once associated, in the minds of the worshippers, with the church at home, and all its hallowed associations; and these reflections tend to subdue the mind, and to make the services more impressive.

> "There is a joy which angels may well prize;
> To see, and hear, and aid God's worship, when
> Unnumbered tongues, a host of Christian men,
> Youths, matrons, maidens, join."

RELIGIOUS SERVICES IN THE CHAPEL.

There must be preaching, with the proper devotional exercises, at least once on every Sabbath day. No chaplain can omit this service, under ordinary circumstances, without gross neglect of duty; and its habitual neglect should lead to the speedy dismissal of the officer, so offending, from the service of the Government. He must PREACH. A few impromptu remarks; a few minutes of rambling talk upon some religious subject once a week, is but religious mockery; and it will not answer for preaching in the chapel. Here the chaplain must bring the highest powers of his intellect into active and vigorous play. He has a peculiar audience before him; in many respects entirely unique and different from all other congregations. Here are the officers of the hospital, most of whom have been accustomed to hear able preaching, and many of them are gentlemen of eminent learning, and accustomed to close analysis and logical deduction; and they will not attend upon the ministrations of a chaplain who habitually neglects all preparation for the chapel service, when he ought to bring the beaten oil into the sanctuary, and produce the results of the closest investigation of the subjects upon which he attempts to speak. But the officers are, appropriately, a part of his parish, and they have a right to his ministrations; and although they should attend as a religious duty, yet, usually, they will not, unless the chaplain makes proper preparation for the service. But they have souls to be saved, or they will be lost. Their influence in the hospital, and in the world, is great; and to lead their souls to Christ, may not only be the means of their salvation, but of incalculable good to others.

A large proportion of the men, too, who compose the present army, are well educated, and from the higher walks of society, and accustomed to good preaching, and expect the same of their chaplain; and although they, also, should attend upon his ministrations as a religious duty, yet they will not, unless he interest and instruct them when they do attend. And some are ignorant, and have not had the advantages of a religious education, and to interest and instruct them, requires an aptness of illustration, and a simplicity of speech which is much more difficult than to explain the same doctrines to the more educated.

These are the usual characteristics of ordinary congregations of worshippers, and they are mentioned, not to apologize for the sinful neglect of attendance upon the ordinances of religion by so many officers and men in the army, but to notice the fact that these characteristics in ordinary congregations are so far felt by pastors, as to call forth, the most serious and thoughtful preparation, so as to adapt their discourses, to all these classes, and to interest and instruct them, and lead them to Christ for salvation; and therefore their existence cannot be ignored by the chaplain.

But the largest part of the congregation in the chapel is peculiar, and differs from all other assemblies of worshippers. It is composed of convalescent soldiers. They are just recovering from the power of disease, or the effects of painful wounds; and many of them, seemingly rescued from the very jaws of death, feel grateful to God for his mercy in sparing their lives. Their consciences are tender, and accessible to the truth. Many of them are inquirers, earnestly seeking to know what they must do to be saved. Others are soon to be returned to duty, and exposed to all the perils of war and the carnage of the battle-field, and they look forward, often, with much anxiety to the issue. Some are bowed down under a weight of affliction by the death of comrades and kindred who have fallen a prey to disease or the casualties of war. Others are in low spirits, and suffering all the horrors of homesickness, and weep at the merest reference to loved ones at home, and long, O! how passionately, to be with them, even for an hour.

To be careless in the preparation to meet such an audience, is criminal. It is spiritual murder, for which the great Head of the Church, if not the

Government, will hold the chaplain to a fearful accountability.

But the sermon, and all the accompanying exercises, should be short. The physical condition of the convalescents imperatively demands this. Directness, earnestness, and brevity, are characteristics which should be carefully studied in all exercises in the chapel.

The themes should be selected with care, and be such as are adapted to this peculiar audience; and all purely denominational tenets and specialities should be carefully guarded against. In the American army, representatives from every denomination and creed are mingled; and upon the great fundamental principles of Christianity, all essentially, agree; and the chaplain will find abundant material in explaining and enforcing such subjects upon the hearts and consciences of his hearers, without entering the domain of polemical theology, or attempting to enforce the peculiar doctrines of any particular denomination. The very attempt to do the latter, will weaken his influence, if not destroy it; and if persevered in, it should demand his immediate dismissal from the service, as being unfitted for the duties of his office.

OTHER RELIGIOUS SERVICES IN THE CHAPEL.

Preaching upon the Sabbath, however, is not the only service demanded. There should be prayer every evening in the chapel, when there is no more formal religious service in it. This exercise should partake, as much as possible, of the nature of family worship; and it will be found to be a most delightful and welcome exercise to the convalescent soldier.

Many of the men, perhaps a majority of them, have been accustomed to family prayers, in their youth, at home; and from habit, if not from religious principles, delight to meet at the altar, and take part in the evening devotions. Here many a stout heart has bowed to the Redeemer's sceptre, and many a careless eye has moistened with tears of penitence, as his mind has wandered back to the years of childhood and youth, and recalled the prayers of sainted parents around, the family altar. Others think of their present homes and of loved ones far distant, who nightly bow around the family altar and implore the blessings of a merciful Providence upon them, and anxiously await their return from the scenes of war; and eagerly, and with heart felt joy, they unite in prayer for God's special blessing and tender care over those loved ones, during their absence from them. The hearts of all are touched; and all are in the happiest mood for profitable meditation, and for receiving lasting religious impressions.

These exercises, as in the family, should be short and to the point. A few stanzas of a hymn should be sung; a few verses of Scripture, read, with an occasional expository or practical remark; a short, earnest prayer offered; and concluded with the benediction.

There should, also, be a weekly lecture, and social prayer-meeting in the chapel. It has been found advantageous in nearly all churches to have the weekly lecture and prayer-meeting in the congregation. They instruct the mind, and invigorate the spiritual graces, and their influence upon the religious status of the congregation is very great.

Equally, and even more important to the convalescents, is the weekly lecture, and the social prayer-meeting. They need instruction; they need admonition and warning; and the chaplain will find the weekly lecture and prayer-meeting powerful means of usefulness and of permanent good to the men under his care. The lecture should be lucid, direct, earnest, and brief. In the social prayer-meeting, there should be as little formality as possible. All should feel at liberty to participate in the exercises, and all should study to be brief.

CHAPTER III.

THE CHAPLAIN IN THE WARD.

> O! to be brought to Jesus' feet,
>   Though sorrows fix me there,
> Is still a privilege; and sweet
>   The energies of prayer,
> Though sighs and tears its language be,
> If Christ be nigh and smile on me.
>
> CONDER.

THE chaplain's duties in the ward, among sick, wounded, and dying men, are among the most difficult and varied of any class of duties of the Christian ministry; and in view of them, any one may well ask, "who is sufficient for these things?"

Here lies a man who had been a professor of religion prior to entering the army, and who has been carried away, amidst the temptations of the camp, to the neglect of his religious duties, and to the commission of numerous and heinous sins. Since the hand of affliction has been laid upon him, the Spirit has revealed to his mind the enormity of his ingratitude and sins, and he is deeply distressed about them, and longs for the Christian conference and prayers of the chaplain. He must remember from whence he has fallen, and repent, and do his first works, and be kindly admonished of the danger and sin of relapsing again into such a state of forgetfulness of God, and of religious duty.

Here, at the point of death, lies a man, who has led a wild and wicked life, and is still utterly careless and unconcerned about the eternal interests of his soul. Will the tender entreaty of the chaplain bring his mind to the contemplation of his awful condition, "having no hope, and without God in the world"? Will the mellow voice of earnest supplication and prayer, awaken in him a sense of his need of a Saviour? May not the tender enunciation of the earnest invitations of the gospel to sinners, arrest his attention, and lead him to accept the proffered salvation? Is he in a fit condition to converse? Shall he be let alone in the hardness of his heart, to die in his sins?

Such are some of the questions which involuntarily start in the chaplain's mind as he stands by his bedside, contemplating his sad condition, and marking the sure and deadly advance of disease upon his frail system. In an hour, that heart will throb no more, and the doom of the soul will be sealed for ever. Oh! that hour! It must be improved, and its proper improvement will tax the highest skill and the most mature judgment of any chaplain; and yet it is a case of almost daily occurrence in every hospital in the government.

There lies a heroic Christian warrior, in all his sublime confidence in God. In early youth he enlisted under the banner of the cross, and swore true allegiance to the great Captain of his salvation; and in all these years, he has maintained a good warfare, and fought many a well-contested battle, and by divine grace, has been triumphantly sustained in every conflict,

> "Look at him
> Who reads aright the image on his soul,
> And gives it nurture like a child of light.
> His life is calm and blessed, for his peace,
> Like a rich pearl beyond the diver's ken,
> Lies deep in his own bosom."

Prayer and praise are in his every breath, and Christian converse with the chaplain his delight; and with him, the chaplain will love to linger. The wounded warrior's fund of religious experience, and his sublime trust and profound resignation to the will of God, react upon his own spiritual graces, and quicken and strengthen their growth.

Here is a skeptic, there an inquirer, concerning whose treatment the reader is referred to Chapter V. of this volume.

To-day, the ward is quiet, and the chaplain is alone with the patients and their attendants; to-morrow, there is much confusion; mopping the floor, dressing wounds, inspection, receiving or transferring patients, and the like; what shall the chaplain do?

These are among the daily scenes of the chaplain in the ward, and he must exercise his most mature judgment in their management. He must have cheerfulness, but not frivolity; good humor, but not hilarity. He will find ample scope for the exercise of all the tenderness of the most compassionate nature, as well as all the earnestness of a Christian heart, intent on doing his Master's will. The ward is the most difficult, but one of the most promising fields of usefulness open to the chaplain, and it must be assiduously cultivated by him; and he will find, to his own great encouragement, that the fruits of his faithful labors will be palpable, from day to day, and will greatly redound to the salvation of sinners and the glory of God.

How often he should read the Scriptures and pray in the ward, must depend upon circumstances, and he must exercise his own judgment in each particular case. Where the wards of the hospital are large and few in number, it is desirable that prayer should be offered every day in each; but daily prayer would be impracticable where the wards are small and correspondingly numerous. Prayer comforts the Christian, encourages the inquirer, and is relished even by the irreligious in the ward, and, therefore, must not be neglected by the chaplain; and he must so command his time, and district his wards, as to read the Scriptures and pray in each ward as often as possible. Only a few verses of Scripture should be read at any one time; and care should be exercised in the selection of the portion to be read, so as to be as appropriate as possible to the wants and feelings of the men.

Besides these general prayers in the ward, he will often find it necessary to kneel by the bedside of the dying, of the inquirer, or of the Christian, and offer, in an under tone, a special prayer for that particular individual. This should always be done as often as requested by the individual. Let no excuse be given by the chaplain to a man who asks him to pray with him. It cannot, ordinarily, be neglected without sin. In special cases, the chaplain should suggest prayer, if the patient does not request it; but should it not be agreeable to the patient, he will generally, frankly state the fact, and the chaplain must forego the privilege, and see him at another time.

Chapter IV.

Letter-Writing.

It is generally a delicate duty to advise in relation to familiar correspondence among friends; but in the hospital, the chaplain should not feel any delicacy on account of the private nature of the correspondence itself. Although persons are constantly arriving at the hospital, and departing from it, yet the great influx of patients is, of the sick when the army makes a general advance, and of the wounded after a battle. Upon either of these occasions, it is peculiarly desirable, and indeed necessary to relieve suffering among their families, that the patients should write to their friends promptly on arriving at the hospital.

In many cases the patients will have come from places inaccessible to the mails, or if accessible, they have not been used; and for weeks, perhaps for months, their friends have not heard from them, and are in deep anxiety about them.

A letter from the patient will not only relieve the anxiety of friends, but it will generally be answered by an affectionate letter from them to him, which is often of great benefit to the patient himself. A considerate letter from friends at home, greatly cheers his heart, and tends to arouse and stimulate the system, and conduces to his more speedy recovery. After every great battle, intense anxiety fills every community from which the troops have been drawn; and every family represented in the battle is intensely eager to know the fate of its representative in the conflict. Exaggerated accounts of the number of the killed and wounded are almost always circulated over the country, and these coming to the knowledge of the immediate friends only increase their anxieties, and add to their distress; and therefore, the patients are bound, by every consideration of affection and humanity, to communicate with them at the earliest possible moment; and it is the duty of the chaplain to render them all the aid, in this respect, in his power, and to urge upon them the performance of this sacred duty.

Here will arise the question of furnishing stationery. Most of the men will be without either stationery or money; but, fortunately, in this war, through the noble benevolence of the loyal citizens of the country, the Sanitary and Christian Commissions, and other benevolent associations, are generally able to furnish the hospitals with whatever stationery may be necessary for the purposes indicated; and the chaplain should look after these supplies, and furnish the men with them. And in the want of postage, he should see that all such letters are promptly franked, so as to prevent any delay for want of postage.

Many of the men, on account of their extreme illness or the nature of their wounds, will be unable to write, and as there will be often hundreds of such cases entering the hospital after a battle, what can the chaplain do? It will be physically impossible for him to write the letters himself and attend to his other professional duties; and ordinarily, it would not be desirable to take so much of his valuable time from the appropriate duties of ministering to their spiritual wants; but he will generally find convalescents who will cheerfully write for their comrades, and he need only request the service, to have it duly performed. In some cases it may be found necessary to call to this labor other volunteer writers, who should go from bed to bed through the whole hospital, and give every one an opportunity of communicating with his friends.

In many cases, the patients will hesitate to inform their friends that they are sick or wounded, under a false idea that it will unnecessarily alarm them, and only increase their anxiety rather than relieve them; and it may be necessary to explain the present anxiety of friends, and to urge them to write.

Uncertainty of the event amidst expected calamities, is one of the most trying and harassing feelings which afflict the friends of the soldier; and while it is unnecessarily indulged in by the friends, yet it can only be prevented by frequent correspondence, and a fair statement of the actual state of the health, or the nature of the wound. In this matter, as in all others, the soldier should be frank and honest in the statement of his case. It is a false system of morality which teaches it to be right to falsify, in regard to the state of health to those to whom, above all others, the patient is bound by every consideration of affection and honor, to be candid and truthful. Truth is purity; falsehood, however disguised, is corruption. Truth honors all men; falsehood debases all.

The chaplain is constantly importuned, when writing for the patients, to state that he is much better than he really is, and that his wounds are much less serious than they really are; but he must refuse: not to write, but to falsify. Let him write the truth, temperately and faithfully, and the friends will thank him for it, and an approving conscience will bless him through life.

Chapter V.

Treatment of Cases of Special Religious Interest.

THE faithful chaplain will always have some cases of special religious interest in the hospital. "Whom the Lord loveth, he chasteneth," says the apostle; and sickness and wounds are often the means of bringing the soul to the serious contemplation of religious truth, and of its personal relation and obligations to God.

One class of such patients may be designated as inquirers, in the religious sense of the word. They are cases of deep and thrilling interest. The Spirit of God moves upon their hearts; he calls them to repentance, and to filial trust in Christ. It may be the turning point of their lives. They may now become the true followers of Christ; or, by grieving away the Spirit, they may be left, as Ephraim joined to his idols, to irretrievable anguish and woe. The chaplain cannot be too careful and vigilant in the treatment of such cases. God will hold him to a fearful accountability for the proper treatment of the inquirer, under such deeply solemn and impressive circumstances. God, in his providence, has placed the chaplain in his office, to direct the benighted wanderer home, as well as for the edification of his people; and as one inquires the way thither, woe be unto him who either misguides him, or, by his indifference, suffers him to pursue the paths of sin, to the loss of his soul.

To direct the inquirer is no easy task. There will be something special in almost every case; something which causes the sinner to hesitate, and which keeps him from Christ; something which begets false hopes and fears, which greatly harass his soul. No specific rules can be given for the treatment of such cases, but the chaplain must try to ascertain what the difficulties are, and to remove them. It will not do always to depend upon the impromptu thought to direct the sinner, and to meet his difficulties. What would be thought of a physician who, in cases of great moment, would give the patient but a passing glance, and prescribe accordingly? How carefully does the faithful physician study each case under his treatment, and especially those of great complication and of imminent danger to the life of the patient! In cases of amputation, how carefully he examines the limb, and where it is practicable, how eagerly he seeks the opinions of other eminent surgeons, before he applies the knife. This is right; it is commendable. And if this is so important, when pertaining to the body, how much more important correctly to understand the difficulties, and appropriately to apply the remedies, in matters pertaining to the soul.

In most cases of inquiry, and especially where the inquirer labors long under a sense of his sins without finding relief in an humble faith in Christ, it will be advantageous for the chaplain to make brief notes of the interview, immediately after visiting the patient, so as to be able to analyze, the case in his study, with a view of meeting its difficulties, and of leading the soul to Christ. In the numerous cases which will be under treatment at the same time in large military hospitals, it will be difficult, if not impossible, for the chaplain, without such notes, to recollect the peculiarities of individual cases, so as to make the necessary preparation to meet the difficulties. Such notes, also, may be of great use to the chaplain in after years, in the treatment of similar cases; and through the press, they may be made of lasting benefit to the Church and the religious world.

In all military hospitals, each surgeon is required to prepare brief notes of the manner of treating important cases which, come under his professional care; and at distant posts, to collect such facts and statistics in regard to local disease, climatology, the health of the troops, &c., as he may be able to obtain. These notes are carefully preserved in the archives of the nation, and as many of them as may be of permanent use are, from time to time, condensed by order of the Surgeon-General, and published by Congress for the benefit of the profession and the world.* And there is no good reason why the chaplain should not be required to keep an accurate account of the treatment of special cases in his professional duties. They might be of as much importance to the world as those of the surgeon; and they would often be of great and permanent benefit to the profession. At all events, the chaplain should prepare such notes during the treatment of the case, for his own aid in the matter at the time, so as to be able faithfully to perform his duty to the suffering men whom God has sent to his spiritual oversight. They will greatly aid him, and he will never regret the time occupied in their preparation.

Another class of patients may be denominated the desponding. In many, perhaps in the majority of such cases, they are true children of redeeming love, and are only under a temporary spiritual cloud, and they will soon again greet the genial rays of the Sun of Righteousness, beaming in all their accustomed effulgence upon them.

---

* Medical Statistics, U. S. Army. 3 vols.

Great care must be exercised in these cases, to ascertain, if possible, the probable spiritual status of the patient; for upon the correct diagnosis, so to speak, of the case, may depend the eternal interests of the soul. Is he a Christian, needing comfort? or is he an unconverted man, needing regeneration? These are inquiries of such vital importance, as to commend themselves to the most serious consideration of the chaplain, whenever he meets with such cases.

Among the more prominent characteristics of the despondency of the true believer, may be mentioned, a habitual mourning the absence of the comforting influences and graces of the Spirit; whereas the mere nominal Christian's grief will be more transient, and less clearly defined. The true believer has an abiding faith and confidence in the power and willingness of God to remove his darkness, and restore unto him the joy of His salvation; but the nominal Christian is easily discouraged, and his fitful. The real Christian is regular and constant in prayer; whilst the unconverted will usually pray only on special occasions, and in times of threatening calamity. The believer knows that reformation must begin in the heart, and so expresses himself; the unregenerated man begins with mere external reformation, by lopping off the more flagrant sins of his life; and he not unfrequently mentions many of his moral virtues as a kind of an offset to such sins.

By these, and similar characteristics, the chaplain will generally be able to distinguish the true believer from the unconverted and mere nominal professor; and having made up his mind on that point, he is prepared to give such instruction as will be best adapted to the patient.

In Christian experience, as well as in every department of knowledge, every effect must have an adequate cause; and when the chaplain stands by the bedside of a child of God, and sees him overwhelmed with spiritual darkness and despondency, he must consider the causes which may have led to this state of mind. The state of the body—its weakness and nervousness—sometimes seems to exert such an influence as to becloud the spiritual perception, and overwhelm the soul in despondency. Sometimes this darkness seems to be simply an act of the Divine Sovereignty. As in the natural world, God, at his sovereign pleasure, sends the sunshine and the shade, so in the spiritual; and the believer can only respond, even in his darkest moments, "Even so, Father, for so it seemeth good in thy sight." But, no doubt, the most fruitful cause of such despondency, is his own unfaithfulness, and his unnecessary and unreasonable yielding to the temptations with which he has been surrounded.

These causes, so far as applicable to the patient, must be explained to him; and in the full acknowledgment of God's supreme sovereignty over him, let him betake himself to importunate prayer, for the cleansing power of the Holy Spirit upon the heart. "Create in me a clean heart, O God," was the fervent prayer of the Psalmist, when he felt the sensible withdrawal of the gracious influences of the Spirit from him; and every Christian may safely imitate his example in this respect. If he gets no relief by these exercises, it is often best to treat him as an ordinary inquirer. He will soon find himself upon familiar ground; and as soon as his former processes are recalled, he will begin to realize their nature, and with such realization, all the clouds will usually disappear, and the soul obtain peace and spiritual joy.

The unconverted must be impressed with the fact, and taught to trust in the mercy of Christ, and his power and willingness "to save them to the uttermost that come unto God by him, seeing he ever liveth to make intercession for them."

Another class of special cases will be skeptics and infidels, who will desire to converse upon the subject of religion; some of them from the love of controversy, some from a vain desire to see what the chaplain can say on such subjects as they will propound, and some again from a desire to know the truth, and with an honest intention to follow it, whenever they may be able to understand it.

It will require much skill to manage and direct this class of objectors, whatever may be their motives for entering into the conversation.

To meet them, the chaplain should keep himself fully posted on the evidences of Christianity, and the NEGATIONS of infidelity. Sometimes an exhibition of the utter negation of all good, by every principle of infidelity, will find its proper lodgment in the mind of the objector, and bring him to reflect seriously upon subjects which he has so slightly examined.

Mere controversy should never be indulged in by the chaplain; but he is bound to be always ready to give an answer to every man that asketh him a reason of the hope that is in him. He should strive to be able to do this in such a logical form, and by such a lucid statement of the principles involved, as at once to silence the caviler, and instruct the honest objector, and to lead both to the discovery of the truth as it is in Jesus. Let the great doctrines of salvation be constantly held up to his view, and kindly and earnestly pressed upon his consideration, and his captiousness will soon vanish, and his thoughtlessness will give place to serious meditation. The author has treated a number of cases of infidelity in this way, and several have been hopefully converted. Christ, and him crucified, is the best argument against infidelity.

CHAPTER VI.

THE DYING; THE DEAD, AND THEIR BURIAL.

THE friends of deceased soldiers usually think their affliction peculiarly severe, from the fact that their loved ones have died away from home, and without the constant and endearing attention of their own tender hands, and the faithful ministration of their own beloved pastor.

"How was he cared for?" "What were his feelings in view of death?" "What were his prospects for eternity?" "Did he seem prepared to die?" These are among the earnest inquiries which the choked utterances of heaving breasts, will press upon the chaplain; and upon the nature of his answer will greatly depend the measure of their grief.

It is, therefore, clearly the duty of every chaplain, as far as possible, to ascertain the feelings and prospects of the dying, in view of the solemn event before him, and to make a note of it for future reference. It is also his duty to afford the dying soldier an opportunity of sending any message to his friends and kindred, which he may desire to communicate. The parting word! that last message of affection! Oh! if it can only be known by the friends, it tends greatly to bind up the lacerated heart-strings which bleed at every pore, when the loved one is called away.

> "Tell my mother that her other sons shall comfort her old age.
>
> *　　　　*　　　　*　　　　*
>
> Tell my sister not to weep for me, and sob with drooping head,
> When the troops are marching home again, with glad and gallant tread,
> But to look upon them proudly, with calm and steadfast eye,
> For her brother was a soldier, and not afraid to die."

In large military hospitals, where many often die nearly at the same hour, this may not always be practicable; but it should always be attempted, and the opportunity given to as many as possible.

And in every case of death, the chaplain should immediately inform the nearest kin of the sad event, and give a brief statement of the cause of his death, and his preparation for it, as far as known; and any message which he may have left for his friends; or any other facts which he may deem it desirable to communicate, and which may tend to alleviate their sorrow. This is a most humane and Christian duty; and in the hands of a chaplain, whose heart is keenly alive to the sufferings of absent friends, and who has been careful in ascertaining the feelings and prospects of the dying, it affords rare opportunities for mitigating sorrow, and for active ministerial usefulness.

Such letters are read and re-read by scores of sorrowing friends, and they cannot be too carefully written, or too full in the narration of facts which may tend to comfort the afflicted, and lead the minds of all to Christ, the great fountain of all comfort and consolation.

As many die soon after entering the hospital, and many others suddenly and unexpectedly, to be able to communicate even the fact of his death to the nearest kin, it will be necessary to keep a Chaplain's Register. A suitable ruling for such a register is here indicated.

Chaplain's Register of the Sick and Wounded at .... Hospital.		
Remarks.		
State.		
County.		
Post-office of nearest kin.		
Relationship of.		
Name of nearest kin.		
Conjugal Condition.		
Nativity.		
Religious Belief.	*	
Residence before enlistment.		
Age.		
Company.		
Regiment or Corps.		
Rank.		
Name.		
Admitted.		

[* A communicant.]

[This form is designed to cover two pages of the Register.]

Some facts will be elicited by this form which are unnecessary for the chaplain's use, such as nativity, age, &c., although it may often be desirable for even these to be known by him; but they are necessary to complete the burial record,* as required by existing regulations; and this is the most convenient form and place for the data to be recorded. The amount of writing which such a register requires, cannot be done by the chaplain in person, but it must be done by the clerical force of the hospital, or by convalescents; but the record should be under his immediate direction, and kept as accurately as possible, and should contain the names of all the patients in the hospital.

---

* RECORD OF DEATH AND INTERMENT.

Name and number of person interred, ...
Number and locality of the grave, ...
Hospital number of the deceased, ...
Regiment, rank, and company, ...
Conjugal condition. (and if married, the residence of the widow,) . . . . . .
Age of the deceased, ...
Nativity, ...
Reference and remarks, ...
Date of death and burial, ... *

With such a register, and his private notes, the chaplain will not, ordinarily, find any difficulty in communicating with the nearest kin, in case of the death of a patient. Such a record will often be an invaluable aid to the Government, and to friends in tracing the identity of many soldiers who have died in the service, and of whom the friends have lost all trace, and thus facilitate the settlement of their accounts, and the pensions of those who are justly and legally entitled to the same.

The column of "religious belief" will greatly aid the chaplain in the performance of his duties, and will afford valuable statistics to the corps, which will be of permanent interest to the profession. The [*] as indicated, is attached to those only who are in full membership with the denomination indicated in the column of "religious belief."

The burial of the dead must be carefully attended to. It was clearly the design of Congress, in creating the office of Hospital Chaplain, and of the President in recommending the measure, to afford to the sick and wounded soldiers of the nation, the consolations of religion in their sickness, and in the case of death, a Christian burial; and this duty, therefore, cannot be neglected by the chaplain. It is alike the dictate of religion and humanity, to treat the dead with the utmost respect, and proper solemnity; and, as far as possible, to console the immediate relatives, who most deeply feel the loss of their friends. It is sufficiently painful to them to think that the cherished idol of their hearts has made his grave among strangers, where the night winds whisper no requiem of love, and the dew-drops mingle not with the falling tear of affection, without the additional reflection, that he has been hastily buried without one thought of them, or the usual services of our holy religion. Rather let it be known, that every man who dies in the service of his country receives an appropriate Christian burial. If the place of burial be at an inconvenient distance, the services may be held at the hospital before the removal of the remains; but a burial service should be had over the remains of every one who dies in the hospital, and it is the imperative duty of the chaplain to attend to it.

The hour of burial should always be stated in the requisition for his burial, for the escort, &c.; and at that hour the chaplain should always attend; and no body should be given to the undertaker at any other time, or without the knowledge of the chaplain. It is his right to demand this, and no surgeon in charge will refuse to make the necessary regulations in regard to it, where the chaplain is faithful in the performance of his obligations in regard to the burial of the dead.

The regulations provide for an escort for every man who dies in the military service of his country; and, under ordinary circumstances, such an escort can always be obtained, by the proper requisition of the surgeon in charge; and it should always be in attendance, when practicable, and accompany the remains to the place of burial, and commit them to the grave with the military honors to which they are justly entitled.

CHAPTER VII.

GAMES—READING MATTER.

It is exceedingly desirable, that the minds of the sick, and especially of the convalescents, should be kept profitably occupied. They will not be idle; and if not otherwise occupied, they seize upon cards, backgammon, checkers, chess, &c. Games which are purely scientific, as chess, checkers or draughts, &c., are, perhaps, admissible for amusement; but cards, and all games of chance, tend to demoralize the mind, and should be prohibited in the hospital. They are not admitted into the chamber of the very sick in private families, even where they are used in health, and they are just as much out of place in the hospital as in the family.

It would greatly shock the moral feelings of the friends of a dying soldier to find on entering the ward, by the side of the dying man, a number of his comrades busily occupied with the exciting throws of the dice, or playing a game of eucre or whist, and altogether unconcerned about the condition of the dying man. There is always much gambling among soldiers, wherever cards are allowed. The stakes are often simply for cigars, lemonade, oysters, &c., but however trivial the stake, or the penalty of losing the game, it is nevertheless gambling, which cannot be justified on any correct principles of morality. It is unnecessary to give any dissertation upon gambling. "He who gambles is damned," is a fearful declaration; but observation upon the general end of gamblers will convince any one of its general truthfulness.

But the practice of card-playing is so repellant to the moral sense of the religious community; so harassing to the feelings of religious soldiers who are sick and wounded, when practised in their presence; to say nothing about the inherent evil of the practice itself, that it should be prohibited altogether in the hospital.

How, then, can the minds of the patients be occupied? BY READING. There are, comparatively, but few men in the army who cannot read. It is the chaplain's duty to endeavor to provide the hospital with reading matter. The religious community are measurably alive to the importance of this matter; and through the liberality of the people, and the agencies of the Bible Societies, Boards of Publication, and other means, the chaplain will ordinarily be able to secure a reasonable supply of reading matter for the hospital.

It is not desirable that it should all be religious matter. The religious should predominate, but history, biography, and miscellaneous reading, should be found in every ward, so as to supply the wants, and give entertainment to all.

The books should all be labelled, before being distributed through the wards. The following label is in use by the writer, and it has been found serviceable, and answers the purposes intended.

This Book is not to be taken from the Hospital.

When read, return it to the Chaplain, or attendant.

The attendants must be instructed to return the book as soon as read, to the library case, or to the librarian, when there is such an officer, so that it can be given to others who may desire to read it. It is desirable to have a librarian to look after the books, and attend to their proper distribution through the hospital; and the chaplain will seldom be at a loss to procure a competent man, from among the convalescents, who will cheerfully attend to the duties of such an office, during his stay in the hospital; and when he leaves, his place can be supplied by another.

Bibles and Testaments should be distributed through the several wards, and should at all times be accessible to the patients. They should never be removed from the ward, and should contain the following label:

> **This Book is not to be taken from this Ward.**

The chaplain will give special attention to this matter, and afford every opportunity which any one may desire, to read the Holy Scriptures.

Besides procuring books, and attending to their proper distribution through the hospital, the chaplain should endeavor to put a tract or religious newspaper into the hands of every patient who is able to read, at least every Sabbath morning.

In the judicious selection of these, and having a sufficient variety to vary the subjects, by giving a different one to each of the several patients in the ward, he will be able to furnish an abundance of reading matter for the entire day, and perhaps much which will be read and re-read during the current week.

Religious newspapers are most relished by the patients generally; and by making known to the religious world the wants of the hospital in this respect, it is hoped the means of furnishing the newspapers will generally be supplied to the editors, by the benevolent in the churches. Distributing such reading matter on Sabbath morning, serves the double purpose of affording excellent and profitable instruction to the mind, and prevents much worldly conversation and employment, which would otherwise occupy the minds of the patients, and especially of the convalescents in the hospital.

Besides the distribution of reading matter through the wards, as indicated in the preceding pages, a reading-room for the convalescents is very desirable. In it should be found some of the leading daily papers, from the different sections of the country; monthlies, quarterlies, and miscellaneous literature. The newspapers should be carefully kept on files, so as to preserve them, and prevent them from being carried out of the reading-room. No one should be allowed to destroy any paper, or take any thing from the room, which is designed for its exclusive use. Talking, and other noise, in the reading-room, should be prohibited, and the rules for its management should be rigidly enforced.

CHAPTER VIII.

DISCIPLINE.

DISCIPLINE is one of the essential requisites of the army, and must be enforced in the hospital, as well as in the camp. The general rules and police regulations of the hospital are made by the surgeon in charge, and must be obeyed by all connected with the hospital, whether officers or enlisted men; and the chaplain will give his personal influence in enforcing the regulations,—and he may often find it proper and prudent to caution the patients against the violation of them, and especially such of them as pertain to the moral and religious conduct of the men. He cannot witness the open violation of such regulations without a remonstrance, or a rebuke from him, and command the respect of the men. In the army, men expect discipline, and any officer who neglects it, will lose the respect and confidence of the very men whom he indulges. The chaplain is no exception to this general principle, in regard to regulations pertaining to morals and religion, which he is expected to respect, and to be solicitous for their due enforcement. There are some regulations pertaining to this subject, with which he should be familiar. The President's General Order* respecting the observance of the Sabbath day in the Army and Navy; the Articles of War in relation to attendance upon Divine service;* the use of profane language;†

---

*

EXECUTIVE MANSION,
Washington, D. C, *Nov.* 15, 1862.

The President, Commander-in-chief of Army and Navy, desires, and enjoins the orderly observance of the Sabbath by the officers and men in the military and naval service. The importance, for man and beast, of the prescribed weekly rest, the sacred rights of the Christian soldiers and sailors, a becoming deference to the best sentiment of a Christian people, and a due regard for the Divine will, demand that Sunday labor in the army and navy be reduced to the measure of strict necessity.

The discipline and character of the national forces should not suffer, nor the cause they defend be imperiled by the profanation of the day or name of the Most High. At this time of public distress, adopting the words of Washington in 1776, "men may find enough to do in the service of God and their country, without abandoning themselves to vice and immorality." The first general order issued by the Father of his Country after the Declaration of Independence, indicates the spirit in which our institutions were founded, and should ever be defended. "The general hopes and trusts that every officer and man will endeavor to live and act as becomes a Christian soldier, defending the dearest rights and liberties of his country." ABRAHAM LINCOLN.

* ART. 2. It is earnestly recommended to all officers and soldiers diligently to attend Divine service; and all officers who shall behave indecently or irreverently at any place of Divine worship, shall, if commissioned officers, be brought before a

drunkenness,[‡] &c., which have an important bearing upon the moral and religious interests of the soldiers, and should be obeyed in the hospital; and the chaplain should give every aid in his power to the surgeon in charge in enforcing them. And if the commanding officer should neglect the moral discipline of the hospital, the regulations prescribe the remedy.

But the chaplain should ever recollect that there is a wrong way to do right; and that he, above all other officers, is expected to exercise the utmost prudence and discretion. Men in this country have, generally, so far felt the power of Christianity, and imbibed its truths, as to have a proper sense of right

---

general court-martial, there to be publicly and severely reprimanded by the President; if non commissioned officers or soldiers, every person so offending, shall, for his first offence, forfeit one-sixth of a dollar, to be deducted out of his next pay; for the second offence, he shall not only forfeit a like sum, but be confined twenty-four hours: and for every like offence, shall suffer and pay in like manner; which money, so forfeited, shall be applied by the captain, or senior officer of the troop or company, to the use of the sick soldiers of the company or troop to which the offender belongs.

[†] ART. 3. Any non-commissioned officer or soldier, who shall use any profane oath or execration, shall incur the penalties expressed in the foregoing article: and a commissioned officer shall forfeit and pay for each and every such offence, one dollar, to be applied as in the preceding article.

[‡] ART. 45. Any commissioned officer who shall be found drunk on his guard, party, or other duty, shall be cashiered. Any non-commissioned officer or soldier so offending, shall suffer such corporal punishment as shall be inflicted by the sentence of a court-martial.

and wrong, and of self-government; and when appealed to as men of honor, will generally yield to their convictions and obey all needful restraints; and it is only necessary to invoke the penalties of the regulations, and of the rules of the hospital, when they cannot be otherwise restrained.

Theoretically, hospital discipline is a very knotty subject, and the abstract question will not here be discussed, but practically, with the exercise of common sense on the part of the officers, it is a very easy and simple matter. Let the officers themselves strictly obey the regulations and the rules of the hospital, and treat the men with kindness and courtesy, and rigidly enforce discipline, and they will always secure the respect and esteem of the men, and receive from them a prompt and willing obedience to all just and reasonable demands.

There may sometimes be matters peculiar to certain localities or hospitals, which affect the moral and religious interests of the hospital, and which it is desirable to have properly regulated, and for which the rules of the hospital make no provision. In such cases it is the privilege and duty of the chaplain to call the attention of the surgeon in charge to the matter, and make such suggestions, as in his professional judgment, are right and necessary. If the suggestions are judicious, in all ordinary cases, he will make the requisite regulations. He may not be a Christian, and may not view it from the high standpoint of Christian duty, yet he feels an interest in the well-being of the men, and he has a professional reputation to be sustained, and it will always be to his interest, as it will generally be his pleasure, to bring up the hospital to as high a degree of perfection as possible, both in respect to the health of the men, and to their discipline and moral status; and he will, therefore, cheerfully coöperate with a judicious chaplain in his appropriate work, and in maintaining a high moral standard for the conduct of the men.

CHAPTER IX.

MATTERS FOREIGN TO THE OFFICE OF CHAPLAIN.

A THOUSAND and one matters, which are entirely foreign to the duties of his office, will be constantly pressed upon the attention of the chaplain, and which he will do well to avoid. He is not a common-carrier, an express-man, a post-boy, a claim-agent, a paymaster, a commissary, a quartermaster, an undertaker, a banker, a ward-master, a hospital-steward, or a surgeon; and he must not assume the duties of these several officers, although they will be constantly urged upon him.

As a rule, he should avoid all matters not legitimately pertaining to the duties of his office. This should be the rule; and attention to matters beyond this should be rare exceptions, and these exceptions should only pertain to matters which may be required to be done for the comfort and convenience of the men, and for which no provision has been made, and which do not legitimately belong to any other officer or attaché of the hospital. He will exercise a just discrimination and proper judgment in relation to these; but a heart in full sympathy with suffering men, and a mind intent on doing good, mitigating suffering, and preventing future misery, will readily elect what, in individual cases, should be done by him, and what must be left for others to perform.

From his high office as a Christian minister, and his constant mingling with the men, they confide more in him than in any other officer of the hospital; and they will be constantly pressing him with various inquiries about matters both within his appropriate duties and beyond them, and with statements of their grievances, real and imaginary. To all such inquiries and complaints he should listen patiently, and should kindly refer the patient to the appropriate officer for information or redress. Care should be taken not to encourage a discontented or complaining spirit; but where there appears to be good grounds for complaint, in any matter connected with the hospital, he should report the facts, as far as known to him, to the surgeon in charge, who will correct the abuses where they exist, and remove all just cause of complaint.

There should always exist the utmost harmony of feeling, as there is a community of interest, between the chaplain and the surgeon in charge, so that the one may always feel at ease in speaking of such complaints, and the other be assured that it is done from proper motives.

PART II.

REGIMENTAL AND POST-CHAPLAIN.

Chapter I.

The Regimental Chaplain— Appointment.

THE existing laws, in relation to regimental chaplains, are as follows: "That there shall be allowed to each regiment one chaplain, who shall be appointed by the regimental commander, on the vote of the field-officers and company commanders on duty with the regiment at the time the appointment shall be made. [*The chaplain so appointed must be a regularly ordained minister of a Christian denomination, and shall receive the pay and allowances of a captain of cavalry*—REPEALED,] and shall be required to report to the colonel commanding the regiment to which he is attached, at the end of each quarter, the moral and religious condition of the regiment, and such suggestions as may conduce to the social happiness and moral improvement of the troops."[*]

"Sec. 7. *And be it further enacted,* That one chaplain shall be allowed to each regiment of the army, to be selected and appointed as the President may direct: *Provided,* That none but regularly ordained ministers of some Christian [religious] denomination shall be eligible to selection or appointment."[†]

"Sec. 8. *And be it further enacted,* That so much of section nine of the aforesaid act, approved July twenty-second, eighteen hundred and sixty-one, and of section seven of the 'act providing for the better organization of the military establishment,' approved August third, eighteen hundred and sixty-one, as defines the qualifications of chaplains in the army and volunteers, shall hereafter be construed to read as follows: That no person shall be appointed a chaplain in the United States army who is not a regularly ordained minister of some religious denomination, and who does not present testimonials of his present good standing as such minister, with a recommendation for his appointment as an army chaplain from some authorized ecclesiastical body,

---

[*] An act to authorize the employment of volunteers to aid in enforcing the laws and protecting public property, approved July 22, 1861; section 9.

[†] An act providing for the better organization of the military establishment, approved August 3, 1861. [This pertains to the regular army.]

or not less than five accredited ministers belonging to said religious denomination.

"Sec. 9. *And be it further enacted,* That hereafter, the compensation of all chaplains in the regular or volunteer service, or army hospitals, shall be one hundred dollars per month and two rations a day when on duty:[*] and the chaplains of the permanent hospitals, appointed under the authority of the second section of the act approved May twentieth, eighteen hundred and sixty-two, shall be nominated to the Senate for its advice and consent, and they shall in all respects fill the requirements of the preceding section of this act relative to the appointment of chaplains in the army and volunteers, and the appointment of chaplains to army hospitals, heretofore made by the President, are hereby confirmed: and it is hereby made the duty of each officer commanding a district or post containing hospitals, or a brigade of troops, within thirty days after the reception of, the order promulgating this act, to inquire into the fitness, efficiency, and qualifications of the chaplains of hospitals or regiments, and to muster out of service such chaplains as were not appointed in conformity with the requirements of this act, and who have not faithfully discharged the duties of chaplains during the time they have been engaged as such.

---

[*] And forage in kind for one horse. Section 2, Act July 17, 1862.

"Chaplains employed at the military posts, called 'chaplain's posts,' shall be required to reside at the posts; and all chaplains in the United States service shall be subject to such rules in relation to leave of absence from duty, as are prescribed for commissioned officers of the United States army stationed at such posts."[*]

Every chaplain appointed under section nine of the act of July 22, 1861, is required to be mustered into the service by an officer of the regular army, and he is thereafter borne on the field and staff-roll of the regiment. He is also required to furnish the mustering officer with a copy of the proceedings on which he was appointed; and when they are found conformable to the requirements of the law, the mustering officer is required to endorse them, and forward them to the Adjutant-General's office, to be filed with the muster-in-roll.[*]

The manner of appointing regimental chaplains of the volunteer force, under the above provisions of law, is not uniform. On the nomination of the regimental commander, the governors of most of the States commission the chaplains of the regiments of the several States, using the same form of commission which is used by them for any other commissioned officer in the volunteer force; while Indiana

---

[*] Act to define the pay and emoluments of certain officers of the army, &c., approved July 17, 1862.

[*] General Order No. 126, 1862.

and Maryland (and perhaps one other State) do not commission any of the chaplains of the regiments belonging to said States. Wisconsin and Rhode Island commission some, on application of the chaplain, and others are not commissioned; and New Hampshire gives a certificate, in the form of a commission, to the chaplain of each regiment of said State, to hold his office, as such chaplain, during the pleasure of the colonel of the regiment. It is to be regretted that there is this diversity. If the regimental chaplain in the volunteer force is a commissioned officer, all should be commissioned; if he is not, none should be commissioned. Very grave questions may grow out of this diversity, in the case of the chaplain being disabled, or dying in the service, as to the rights of himself or heirs. If he is a commissioned officer, he or his heirs will be entitled to a pension of twenty dollars per month, according to his assimulated rank; if a non-commissioned officer, he will only be entitled to the pension of a private soldier.

The uniform of the chaplain and the requirements in relation to it, have been considered in a former part of the volume,[*] to which the reader is referred.

But his duties, unlike every other officer in the army, are not clearly defined by the department, and hence, he is left much to the exercise of his own judgment as to what his duties are, and how they

---

[*] Part I., Chapter I.

shall be performed. They will be more fully defined in the following chapters, but to faithfully discharge the necessary duties of his high and holy office as a Christian minister, in this anomalous position, requires a higher order of moral, and as much physical courage, as to lead a regiment in the charge against a battery, or to storm the works of an enemy. And yet he must take the responsibility, and meet the issue. He must create his position in the regiment; and he has it in his power to create a lofty and an enviable one. Relying upon his high commission as an ambassador of God, and under all circumstances, however discouraging, courageously and faithfully performing the appropriate duties of his holy profession, in the fear of God, and with an eye single to His glory and the salvation of souls, he will be more loved than any other officer, and as much respected and feared. Courage is a cardinal virtue in the army. Officers and men everywhere respect it, and honor the man who possesses it. They know the anomalous and trying position of the chaplain, and applaud the moral heroism which removes the obstacles and overcomes the difficulties of the office, and respect him the more on that account.

But of all detested things in the army, cowardice is the most despised; and whenever a chaplain of the regiment is seen to be wanting in moral and physical courage, and cowardly skulking away from known duty, his influence is gone. He is a supernumerary attaché to the army, a mere cypher in the regiment; and he might as well return at once to his former duties and field of labor.

CHAPTER II.

PUBLIC RELIGIOUS INSTRUCTION.

THE regiment is the chaplain's congregation or parish, and he should feel as much anxiety and responsibility to give regular and appropriate public instruction to the men, as he would in an ordinary pastoral charge. In fact, when the trials, perils, and temptations of camp-life are considered, there are special reasons for being even more diligent in the performance of his professional duties in the chaplaincy, than in the parish. Every man in the regiment may be said to be in imminent peril. The professors of religion are in peril. They are assailed by the adversary of their souls at every point, and with tremendous power. The old leaven in their hearts begins to work. The corrupt principles of the heart, which may have been kept in subjection for many years, begin to clamor for indulgence. Opportunities for uncleanness and wicked indulgences are abundant; and the gratification of his wicked passions is constantly pressed upon him. The restraints of the family circle are wanting, and measurably so, are those of Christian society. In the camp they may do with impunity what they would not dare to attempt in the presence of their families, or in the midst of a circle of Christian friends at home. The association with openly profane and wicked men, tends to blunt their spiritual perceptions, and to sear the conscience; and the general tendency of the camp is to moral degeneracy; and nothing but the grace of God can prevent the souls of even good men from being carried headlong into sin. The necessity, therefore, for special religious instruction of the professors of religion is much greater in the camp than in the parish; and without it, the most tremendous wreck of character and of Christian professions must result; and the utmost dishonor will be heaped upon the cause of Christ in consequence thereof.

"But if the righteous scarcely be saved, where shall the ungodly and the sinner appear?" With how much more emphasis does the condition of the unconverted call for instruction and warning? No Christian man can contemplate the condition of the irreligious in camp, without painful anxiety. "His heart is deceitful, above all things, and desperately wicked." "It is enmity against God, and is not subject to the law of God." "It is prone to evil as the sparks are to fly upward;" and with all these base principles at work within, and without any counter warfare of holy principles, and having such temptations and opportunities for vice and immorality, he must, in the very nature of things, become more and more hardened in sin, and deeper and deeper sunken in iniquity.

"The soul that sinneth, it shall die;" "except ye be born again, ye cannot enter into the kingdom of heaven." He is, therefore, unprepared to die, and yet constantly exposed to death, and in imminent peril of being for ever lost. The ravages of disease in camp are fearful; the carnage of battle, terrible; and he is exposed to the power of both.

The chaplain cannot look upon these things with indifference or unconcern. He must provide for them to the best of his ability; and one of the most important provisions which he can make, is public instruction—preaching the gospel according to the ordinary public ministration of the sanctuary. At least one sermon, with the appropriate religious services, should be preached, every Sabbath day. Some Sabbaths, more than one service can profitably be held; although, occasionally, circumstances may be such as to render any service impracticable. There should be a definite hour fixed for the service, (immediately after the customary morning inspection is usually the most convenient hour,) and at that hour the church-call should be regularly sounded, and all should repair to the place of worship. He has the right to demand this, and no commanding officer can interfere with it under ordinary circumstances.

No slight excuse can exonerate the chaplain from holding such religious service, and publicly preaching the gospel, upon every Sabbath day. Every consideration which could impel a pastor to be faithful in this respect, in the most important pastoral charge in any community, must press upon him with increased weight and urgency, the necessity of being faithful in the public ministrations of the gospel in the camp.

In the congregation or parish, a weekly prayer-meeting and lecture are found to be important means of grace, and these means will be found equally beneficial in the camp, and should be maintained in every regiment. "Prayer is the Christian's vital breath." He cannot live without it, either at home or abroad. God ordinarily sends blessings upon his children and upon the unconverted, only in answer to prayer; and the more earnest prayer there is in the camp, the more good will, ordinarily, be done.

It is also desirable to have evening prayers in the regiment; and the most appropriate and opportune moment is immediately at the close of dress-parade. Let the colonel order his men to be formed in a square; and then, in a short, earnest, appropriate prayer, let the chaplain commit them to the care of the Almighty. It is the family-prayer of the regiment; and the prayer should have special reference, not only to the wants of the men, but to their families at home. The men will take great pleasure in daily committing, in prayer, their loved ones to the care of Him who knows all their necessities, and is abundantly able to supply them all. God will smile upon such exercises. They would be productive of the happiest effects upon the morals of the regiment, and no doubt would be the means of saving many a precious and immortal spirit.

Where evening prayers are not had at the close of parade, and even where they are, by a little personal effort the chaplain will be able to secure family or evening worship in many, if not all the tents. In almost every tent will be found one or more men who have been accustomed to pray at home; or some who have been converted since entering the army, and who feel the necessity of prayer. By a personal application to the mess, to have prayer by some one of their number in that particular tent, every evening before going to sleep, in numerous instances the matter will be undertaken and performed. He should introduce the exercise by leading, if possible, the first evening himself; and the exercises being once or twice formally introduced, the men will feel less embarrassment in continuing them. Let every chaplain make the effort to introduce these evening prayers, and earnestly press the matter, in a Christian spirit, upon the moral and religious members of the mess, and the happiest results will follow.

A pastor does not usually secure family worship in every family of his congregation, not even of his membership; but this does not deter him from urging the duty upon all heads of families, with a view of securing so valuable a result. So let the chaplain strive with every mess. He may not succeed in all; but he will succeed in some; and the blessed fruits of even one such evening altar, will vastly more than repay him for the effort. He will occasionally find that there is no one of the mess willing to undertake to lead in prayer, while all express a willingness, and even a desire, to have such evening service. The chaplain's duty is then clear. He must fix upon an hour for such prayers, and go himself and lead the devotions. This will soon become a pleasant hour to all; and in time, that mess will have men among them who will cheerfully lead, in the providential absence of the chaplain, and thus, they may be educated by him to lead the devotions regularly every evening.

CHAPTER III.

PASTORAL VISITATION.

THE social principle is one of the most powerful and controlling principles in the human heart; and having been placed there by Providence, for wise and holy purposes, it is the chaplain's duty to make it subserve, as far as he can, the great interests of the Redeemer's kingdom on earth. To this end, he must visit from tent to tent, and become intimately acquainted with the men. He must know them by sight, and be able to recall at once the former history of each. He must learn the localities of their homes; the character and religious standing of their parents, friends, and associates; their former business; their successes and reverses; their education, and so on, as far as these facts can be ascertained, without improperly prying into private matters.

He will thus be able to form a correct idea of their former habits and moral status; will be able to sympathize more fully with them in their troubles and perplexities; will gain their confidence, and be in the most desirable position to communicate instruction. No chaplain can be said to have done his duty, who has been any considerable length of time with his regiment, and does not know the majority of his men personally, and much of the personal history of each. In his intercourse with the men, let him avoid unbecoming familiarity and levity upon the one hand, and unnecessary professional reserve and assumed dignity on the other, and the men will soon respect him as a friend, and confide in him as a brother.

That the facts, which may be elicited from time to time, relating to the personal history of each man, may be the more serviceable to him, the chaplain should keep a private register, containing the name, company, and rank of every man in the regiment, in which to note the facts and incidents of each one's life. This will prevent confusion, and will enable him, at a glance at any name, to recall the facts at pleasure. This register should always be consulted, after it has been considerably filled up, before visiting special cases; and in the preparation of the proper themes of conversation and instruction. No two men are constitutionally alike; and each may require a different treatment to bring him to the same point, and nothing can more aid the chaplain in marking this distinction, and adapting himself to it, than the facts in his register, if they are full and accurate.

Pastoral visitation in the camp, is a field which requires very considerate cultivation. It requires the exercise of his best judgment, both as to the extent of religious conversation at each visit, and the time and manner of introducing the subject, and of leaving it and introducing other matters. Different persons not only require to be differently approached, but the same person is not always alike approachable. Time, place, and circumstances, often greatly change the moods of men, and are, therefore, to be duly considered by the chaplain, so far as may be necessary to adapt himself to the circumstances of men, and his instruction to their wants and necessities.

In this work, as well as in other labor, regularity adds greatly to one's efficiency; and the chaplain should devote a particular portion of each day to this specific work, and adhere to the arrangement as closely as possible. If he leave the matter to mere leisure moments, or occasional opportunity, it will seldom be attempted; and when attempted, it will be feebly done. It requires thought and courage to go forth properly in this work—a courage often higher than is required to stand in battle array, or to march to the cannon's mouth. The latter is done amidst the intense excitement incident to battle; the former is a deliberate assault upon a wily enemy, entrenched behind the breastworks of the prejudices and sinful passions of the heart. Such an enemy is not easily dislodged; and even good men often hesitate to attack him. But he can be dislodged, and the chaplain must not hesitate to make the effort; and if he fails in the first assault, which he often does, he must renew the attack more vigorously, from time to time, until he succeeds in his endeavor.

Often very favorable opportunities will occur for pressing the truth home to the heart, and these are to be diligently improved. If an individual has been sick, and has promised reformation and a dedication of himself to Christ on his recovery, he must be reminded of these promises. If he has made such vows, as is often done, when going into battle, he must be reminded of them when the battle is over.

The foundation for appropriately pressing home religious truth having been laid, in learning his personal history, a great variety of incidents and facts will be suggested, in connection with camp life, peculiarly appropriate to the wants and circumstances of individual cases; and they must be diligently and prayerfully used for the interests of the men. God has, in all ages, honored such agencies as means of leading the soul to him, and this should inspire the chaplain with greater zeal in their use. As he looks over his register, or mingles with the men, from day to day, let him think how many of these noble and brave men may be called to the bar of God in the very next battle, or be early carried away by disease; and it must move his soul to tears to contemplate their spiritual condition, in view of such contingencies. If they die, or are killed, being unregenerated, they die in their sins; and if they are unwarned by him, their blood will be required at his hands. The blood of souls! Let it never stain the chaplain's uniform, or mark the wreck of his own destruction. Let his "present diligence prepare for future, blessedness."

> "But in his duty prompt at every call,
> He watched and wept, he prayed and felt for all;
> And as a bird each fond endearment tries
> To tempt its new-fledged offspring to the skies,
> He tried each art, reproved each dull delay,
> Allured to brighter worlds, and led the way."

CHAPTER IV.

THE SICK AND WOUNDED IN THE CAMP.

THE chaplain should visit the regimental and division hospital daily, and afford the consolations of religion to the sick and dying of his regiment. Men who have been utterly careless upon the subject of religion in health, will welcome the chaplain to their bedside in the hospital, and will listen attentively to his instruction. The Christian who had become cold and formal, if not totally indifferent, will long for his spiritual advice, and an interest in his prayers. The pious wish to converse with him about salvation, and the precious promises of the gospel. All will welcome him, and religious conversation and prayer will be expected from him by all. He will find the hospital one of the most attractive and encouraging parts of his field of labor, and he must diligently cultivate it. For the general particulars of the cultivation of this field, the reader is referred to another part of this volume,* where the subject is more fully presented.

During a battle, the chaplain should be with the surgeons, assisting in caring for the wounded, and affording the consolations of religion to the dying. The excitement and confusion of the hour, and the immediate and pressing physical wants of the wounded, tend to call off the chaplain from his first and highest duty—the spiritual wants of the men—to those duties which more appropriately belong to the stewards and attendants. While it is his duty to do everything in his power to minister to their physical wants, and to mitigate their sufferings, yet he must not forget the spiritual wants of any, and especially of the dying. They may have but a moment to live, and upon the proper improvement of that moment, may hang the eternal destiny of their souls. They must not be neglected by him. They may want to send a dying message to friends; let him hear the message, and as promptly as possible transmit it to them. However much he may desire to do for the body, he must be more solicitous for the soul. It is impossible to determine in advance, how much time to devote to the one, or how little to the other; but a chaplain who fully feels the responsibilities of his office, and whose heart is in full sympathy with the suffering soldiers, will not have much

---

* Part I., Chapter III.

difficulty in determining the point in the practical solution of it.

But if he is detailed, as sometimes he will be, to superintend the fitting up of the general hospital, his duties, for the time being, will be chiefly executive, and he must give his attention exclusively to it. It will tax his time and resources to their utmost; and as the comfort, if not the lives, of hundreds of patients will greatly depend upon its arrangement, supplies, attendants, &c., he cannot be too active and vigilant in requiring everything to be properly done, and the patients to be properly cared for.

The burial of the dead, correspondence with absent friends, &c., have been considered elsewhere, and to which the reader is referred.

Chapter V.

Religious Reading.

A VALUABLE aid to the chaplain, in all his labor, is the religious press; and he should avail himself of this aid as much as possible. The men in camp will generally read anything which is placed in their hands; but care should be taken to have it of a suitable kind, and as attractive as possible. Religious newspapers and tracts are the best adapted to the field. They are read and re-read with avidity; and although they are then generally thrown aside, or sent to their friends, yet their contents have been impressed upon the memory, and will not soon be forgotten. Bound books are excellent where troops are comparatively stationary, but cannot be transported with an active army in the field.

Although religious reading matter cannot always be obtained, yet God, in his merciful providence, has so impressed his people with a sense of the importance of this matter, and has given the means of supplying it, to so many Christian men, and also given them a willing heart to do so, that the chaplain, by keeping himself in constant communication with the various publication houses, and editors of religious newspapers, can, ordinarily, have a measurable supply of reading matter for the regiment. The very effort to obtain it begets, in the hearts of the men, a sense of gratitude, even when but a limited amount is actually obtained, and thus favorably disposes their hearts in his favor, and prepares them for attending more carefully to his ministerial instruction.

It is to be regretted that there is no official provision made for transporting such religious reading-matter from the great military depots to the actual camp in the field. Voluntary societies are doing much, but an official connecting link is much needed. Could there be an assistant quartermaster, or other proper officer, detailed at New York for the sea-coast, Washington, Cincinnati, and St. Louis, to the special duty of receiving such reading-matter as might be donated by the religious world, and with power to forward the same with the other supplies of the army, there would be an ample supply furnished to every regiment. It would be the means of occupying the minds of the men when off duty; it would prevent much gaming, and greatly enhance the social and moral interest of the men, and conduce to good order and discipline in the camp.

The daily reading of the Scriptures by the soldiers, is of paramount importance, and the duty must be earnestly pressed upon them by the chaplain. There are editions of the New Testament, and New Testament and Psalms, such as the *"Dia., 64mo."* of the American Bible Society, which are well adapted to the pocket; and the volume is so light that it can be easily carried. Such a volume should always be carried by every soldier. It is best to have a small pocket in the breast of his shirt, to be used only for the purpose of carrying this little volume, so that he can always have it accessible. If he is on the march, he has in with him; and as he halts by the way, or encamps at eventide, he will often be inclined to read it; and he will always have it in his power to do so. If he is wounded in battle, he may often find a fund of comfort in reading its precious promises, as he lies weltering in his blood, and unable to move from the scene of carnage and death around him.

No man can tell what may be the power of divine truth upon the heart, when read under such circumstances. "Of His own will begat He us with the word of truth, that we should be a kind of first-fruits of his creatures." "Sanctify them through Thy truth: Thy word is truth." It is desirable to have his name, company, rank, regiment, age, height, and complexion, legibly written with ink on the fly-leaf of this little volume; and it will often be the means of identifying him in cases of extreme illness or death, when his identity would not otherwise be ascertained. UNKNOWN is a melancholy inscription to mark the head-board of the soldier's grave; and yet how often, it is the only record which denotes the sleeping brave! It suggests unnumbered sorrows. His parents, brothers, sisters, wife, children, friends!—who can answer their earnest inquiries, or remove their burning suspense as to his fate? What wearisome years of anxiety! Surely anything which can be done to prevent such a calamity, should receive careful attention.

CHAPTER VI.

QUARTERLY REPORT.—CAMP VICES.

THE regimental chaplain of the volunteer force is required "to report to the colonel commanding the regiment to which he is attached, at the end of each quarter, the moral and religious condition of the regiment, and such suggestions as may conduce to the social happiness and moral improvement of the troops."[*] The commanding officer, having so many and varied duties to perform, cannot be expected to know the moral condition of his troops as well as the chaplain, one of whose special duties is to look after this specific matter; and hence the law very properly requires him to report upon this subject to his commanding officer. It is the duty of the latter officer to maintain order, and to elevate his troops to the highest possible perfection of military discipline.

---

[*] Act July 22, 1861, sec. 9.

The efficiency of the army greatly depends upon this. But there can be no high order of discipline among grossly immoral troops; and whatever tends to increase morality among them, aids good discipline; and whatever begets immorality among them, so far destroys their efficiency.

Making the quarterly report, furnishes the chaplain with a rare and important opportunity not only to state the moral and social condition of the troops, but to make official suggestions to his commanding officer, relative to their improvement in these respects. These suggestions are official; they are required by law, and are bound to be such as the chaplain, in the conscientious discharge of his duty, believes to be necessary and proper; and they cannot be construed into impertinence, or an improper meddling, with things which do not belong to him.

Great care should be taken in the preparation of this report. It should be full and replete with facts, and evince thought, and a conscientiousness in the discharge of duty. The suggestions should be carefully matured in his mind before they are embodied in the report, and they should be such as, if possible, to command the assent of every unprejudiced and right-minded person, and to move the heart and convince the judgment of the commanding officer, who has to act upon them, or to take the responsibility of neglecting them.

It is to be regretted that it is not made the duty of the colonel commanding the regiment to forward the quarterly reports of the chaplains to the Adjutant-General's office, to be filed among the Department papers. Were they to be filed, they would perhaps, be more carefully prepared, and they might be of great interest to the future historian, if not of present advantage to the Department.

CAMP VICES.

It is no easy matter, for even religious men, to stem the current of vice and immorality in the camp; and it is no wonder, therefore, that men devoid of the grace of God, often run riot in sin and debauchery. But this current must be stemmed by the religious, and all must be taught to lead a moral life.

Upon these subjects the chaplain must give much instruction, and earnest and solemn warning. "For precept must be upon precept, precept upon precept; line upon line, line upon line; here a little, and there a little." He must impress upon the minds of all, that their sins and immoralities are both heinous in the sight of God, and odious to all good men, and tend to lax discipline and the utter demoralization of the army. Let him plant himself upon his high commission as a minister of the gospel, and fearlessly admonish and exhort, with all long-suffering and doctrine, however humble the position of the offenders, or however high their rank may be. As an ambassador of Christ, he must obey the instructions of the Great Captain who commands him, saying, "Cry aloud, spare not, lift up thy voice like a trumpet, and show my people their transgression, and the house of Jacob their sins." He cannot disobey the command of God. His colonel, or other commanding officer, however debauched in his moral character, does not expect him to disobey it, but will honor him for his faithfulness and his fearlessness in denouncing sin. He must seize upon the most befitting occasions for communicating and enforcing such instruction, and bring to his assistance all the tenderness of his heart and the deepest sympathies of his nature. Let his most pointed rebukes be baptized in tears, and no offence will ever be given. But let him ever bear in mind, that there is no permanent and safe reformation in morals without the regeneration of the soul. There is no true morality without religion. Any system of reformation which falls short of this, is defective, and will utterly fail to accomplish the end it seeks to attain. "Christ, and him crucified," is the great theme for the reformation of the camp. Let the men be justified by His righteousness, and immorality and debauchery will disappear from the camp. Their reformation will be permanent, and their souls will be saved.

CHAPTER VII.

THE POST-CHAPLAIN.

THE posts, not to exceed thirty in number,[*] at which chaplains may be appointed, are designated by the Secretary of War.[†]

The appointment of post-chaplain is made by the Council of Administration; but no one can be appointed who is not a regularly ordained minister of some religious denomination, and who does not present testimonials of his present good standing as such minister, with a recommendation for his appointment as an army chaplain from some authorized ecclesiastical body, or not less than five accredited ministers belonging to said religious denomination.[*] The proceedings of the Council of Administration, pertaining to this appointment, will be immediately forwarded to the Adjutant-General's

---

[*] Act of March 2, 1849.
[†] Act of July 5, 1838.
[*] Act of July 17, 1862.

office. The chaplain is required to reside at the post. The compensation is the same as that of other chaplains in the army—one hundred dollars per month and two rations per day when on duty, and forage, in kind, for one horse.

A chapel should always be attached to the post, where religious services should be conducted with as much regularity as is usual in a congregation or church. The hours for divine service should be fixed, and the church-call should be one of the regular calls of the post. The public services of the chapel should be much the same as in an ordinary congregation, adapting the instruction to the habits and wants of the hearers. This will include preaching, at least, once every Sabbath; prayer-meeting and lecture, at least, once a week; and such additional religious exercises as the chaplain may deem desirable.

Family worship, or evening prayers should be held every evening in the chapel. There are certainly many urgent reasons for insisting on having this service held. The chaplain is required to reside at the post,[*] and can, therefore, easily attend. The soldiers are there, and many of them will esteem it a great privilege to be present. It will recall the scenes of their childhood, and awaken past memories, which will often cause the seed, long since cast into their hearts, to germinate, and to bring forth the

---

[*] Act July 17, 1862.

fruits of faith and holiness unto eternal life. It will beget in the soldiers the habit of daily prayer, which will often follow them, and be continued when they go into the field. The Scriptures, which will be read in their hearing, is food to their souls. The prayers offered, are appointed means for obtaining the blessings asked.

Favorable opportunities are also afforded to the post-chaplain for maintaining a Bible-class, for the systematic study of the Scriptures; and the circumstances of the soldiers imperatively demand the improvement of such opportunity whenever presented. Many of the men are almost wholly ignorant of the great truths of the Bible, and greatly need to be systematically instructed in its sublime doctrines and precepts; and the Bible-class affords a rare opportunity for them to obtain that knowledge which they so much need. It will beget, in many minds, a love for the study of the Scriptures, which they never before experienced, and which will go with them when they leave for other parts of the service, and will often be blessed of God to the salvation of the soul. Let every post-chaplain make an earnest and conscientious attempt to get up and maintain a Bible-class at his post, and God will ordinarily crown him with success, and give him souls for his labor.

There should always be a library of bound volumes of religious and miscellaneous works at every post, for the use of the soldiers. These can ordinarily be obtained, so far as religious books are wanted, by the chaplain, on application to the religious publication houses; and often miscellaneous works can be obtained on application to benevolent persons in the neighborhood, who feel an interest in the post. The library should be under his control; and he can make such rules and regulations in regard to it as he deems necessary, to prevent the books from being abused or lost. He can obtain the services of a soldier, from time to time, to take the immediate oversight of the books, and attend to their proper distribution, and their return to the library.

He should also endeavor to procure a supply of religious tracts and newspapers, sufficient to place one in the hands of every soldier at the post, every Sabbath morning. In some of the posts in the army, there will be no difficulty in procuring these; in others, it may not be possible; but it should always be done when practicable.

In relation to pastoral labor and visitation, camp vices, &c., he is referred to the consideration of the subjects as presented in another part of this volume.[*]

The post-chaplain is also required to perform the duties of schoolmaster. When there are no schools convenient to the post, these duties are very important, and must not be omitted. The children of

---

[*] Part II., Chapter III.

all officers, soldiers, and attachés of the army, serving at the post, have a right to instruction at his hands; and if the number of such should be great, so as to take too much of his time from his ministerial duties, he can generally find an intelligent and competent man in the ranks, who can be temporarily detached to aid him in this duty. But the chaplain is responsible for the proper discharge of the duty; and as it may be the only opportunity, which some of the children may ever have, of acquiring an education, they must be thoroughly and systematically taught.

THE GOVERNMENT EXPECTS ALL CHAPLAINS TO DO THEIR DUTY, CONSCIENTIOUSLY, AND IN THE FEAR OF GOD.

PART III.

AID TO THE CHAPLAIN.

THERE are many ways by which the friends of the soldier may not only render direct and important aid to the chaplain, but the very effort to aid him, and to coöperate with him, will do incalculable good beyond his immediate influence, through the various agencies by which most of their assistance will reach him. Most of these means have been intimated in different parts of this volume, and they are here grouped together with the hope of securing greater attention to them on the part of the public.

The highest good to the soldier is the salvation of his soul; and it is preëminently to this end that all the efforts of the chaplain should be directed. The word of God is the great instrument, in the hands of the Holy Spirit, for the conversion of sinners, and the sanctification of the soul. "Of his own will begat he us with the word of truth." "Sanctify them through thy truth; thy word is truth." Every chaplain can bear testimony to the fact, that the reading of the Scriptures in the army, has been the means of the hopeful conversion of many precious souls, and has done an incalculable amount of good, which only the developments of eternity can fully reveal. The chaplain, therefore, must be abundantly supplied with the Bible, or at least with portions of the same, for the use of the men under his care. He should be able to place copies of the Bible in every ward of the hospital, and to present, at least, a copy of the New Testament and the Psalms to every man in the army. Men treasure those things which are their own; and although the majority of the soldiers love the Bible for its own sake, as the word of God, able to make them wise unto salvation, yet they will doubly prize the volume when they can call it their own. All will read it occasionally. Some, who have never been in the habit of reading it, will read it daily. Wherever it is read, it is so much good seed sown in the heart, which the chaplain has only carefully to cultivate, and it will bring forth an abundant harvest to the glory of God, and the salvation of souls.

So far in the present war, the American Bible Society and its auxiliaries, have been able to respond to the requisitions of chaplains and others, for copies of the Scriptures for distribution in the army. But thousands of these precious volumes are lost by the casualties of war, and must be replaced. Thousands more are wanted for the new recruits; and the drain, therefore, upon the funds of the Society, must be enormous; and the friends of the soldier must be correspondingly liberal in their donations. Let the

Society be specially sustained in view of the vast work which now demands its attention. Every consideration of love, patriotism, philanthropy, and Christianity, appeals to the friends of the soldier to sustain this noble Society in this glorious work.

Religious books and tracts are invaluable aids to the chaplain. Their importance to the men, has been already noticed; and it is proposed in this place to consider only the question of supply. Whilst much, very much, has already been done, yet the demand for such religious reading in the army has been greatly in excess of the supply. Chaplains have been put off with a hundred tracts, when a thousand could have been profitably used by them; and ten volumes have been given, when a hundred were wanted. Men have begged for religious books and tracts, as starving men beg for bread, and have been unable to obtain them.

This has not been owing to any indisposition on the part of the various Boards of Publication to meet the demand. They have seen the importance of the field, and have heard the urgent solicitations, and have been deeply pained to grant but a moiety of the requests which have been made. They are as ready to grant, as the chaplains are to ask, whenever it has been in their power to do so.

But these Boards of Publication, in this respect, are simply the almoners of the people's bounty. They have not given as much as was solicited, because the friends of the soldier have not provided the means. Ordinary contributions have been given to their funds, whilst extraordinary demands have been made for their publications. The demand, however, is a great public necessity, and it will yet become more and more urgent; and the contributions should be correspondingly liberal. During the continuance of the present war, special and liberal donations to the various Boards of Publication should be made, in some measure at least, commensurate with the vastness and importance of the field to be supplied by them; and until this is done, souls must perish for lack of knowledge. The friends of the soldier can greatly aid the chaplain by furnishing the men with a supply of RELIGIOUS NEWSPAPERS. They are sought for with an eagerness, and read with an avidity, which cannot be adequately described to those who have not witnessed their distribution in the hospital and in the camp. They seize them as famishing men seize food, and devour them with as much gusto; and some have actually kissed the hand of the chaplain as he presented a copy of the old family paper to them, and have baptized the sheet with tears of gratitude as they perused its much loved columns.

The author, having urged this matter upon the United States Christian Commission, takes the liberty of quoting its appeal, and earnestly urging its favourable consideration upon every Christian and patriot.

"The soldiers in the field and in the hospitals are eager for religious newspapers. Their own familiar family denominational papers are the most prized of all. They are read from beginning to end, and passed from hand to hand, until quite worn out. They revive home, church, and Sabbath-school associations; keep up the knowledge of passing events, religious and secular; increase intelligence, prevent demoralization, inspire cheerfulness, encourage patriotism, and strengthen heroic resolve; and, above all, present gospel truths in articles terse and attractive, and illustrate their benign power by narratives of conversions, revivals, and hallowed Christian examples of holy living and happy dying.

"The Christian Commission would rejoice to present, by its delegates and chaplains, the best loved paper of each soldier to him every week; but, even if its treasury could bear the expenses, which it would not, the Commission could not devote means contributed for *general purposes,* to the purchase of *denominational papers.* It can be done, however, by special contributions for the purpose, and to this end an appeal is now made to the friends of each and all the religious papers of the land. Let the friends of each contribute to the paper itself directly, all they can afford for the purpose, and the Commission will see that the papers are placed in the hands of the soldiers.

"It is designed that an article similar to this shall appear in every other paper, and thus an appeal be made to the friends of each through its own columns. And the Commission has this special request to make of editors, in behalf of the soldiers, that they will not permit the matter to drop, but call attention to it, from week to week, until a supply is secured in some measure commensurate with the vastness of our army, and the eagerness of our soldiers. * * * *

"Those who may desire to contribute for the purpose of sending —— paper, will please forward the amount to its publishers, who will furnish the papers to the Commission."

Will the friends of the soldier allow him to suffer all the horrors of homesickness and ennui, when these sufferings can be mitigated, and measurably prevented, by occupying his mind with reading matter which is at once so interesting and profitable to him? Shall the souls of the brave defenders of the nation's life be periled, or given over to be eternally lost, when so favorable an opportunity is presented of awakening thoughts of "righteousness, temperance, and judgment to come," which, by the blessing of God, may be the means of leading them to Christ, and securing their everlasting beatitude? Men cannot carefully read such matter as is generally presented in the religious newspapers without being benefitted thereby; and shall not this powerful agency for good be employed in the present perilous times? Shall the chaplain be denied such valuable aid, when it can be afforded him at a comparatively trifling expense? Let the religious and patriotic answer, in the light of Christian duty, and there will be no cause for complaint. Contributions from every quarter, like so many mountain rivulets, will then flow into this vast reservoir; and from thence, distributing streams will flow through the army, to quench the thirst of many a famishing soul, and to gladden many a sorrowing heart.

Besides, a large percentage of these papers, after having been read by the soldiers, will be re-mailed to their friends at home, by whom they will again be read; and thus, this wave of usefulness will roll on from heart to heart, in the vast ocean of humanity, until it will break beyond the bounds of time, and surge for ever in the shoreless ocean of eternity.

There are two great organized agencies or associations, through which the chaplains have received, and are still receiving, material aid, and which are doing an untold amount of good in the army, and ought to be most cheerfully sustained by the contributions of the friends of the soldier. These are the United States Sanitary Commission, and the Christian Commission, already referred to.

The Sanitary Commission is writing its name upon the tablet of living hearts, and it will be held in grateful remembrance beyond the recollection of the present generation. Its agents are found in every corps and division of the army, and in every hospital, with bountiful hands ready to supply the temporal wants of the soldier, and especially to minister to the temporal necessities of the sick and wounded. It has saved thousands of valuable lives by the distribution of its stores; and thousands more, by its influence upon the sanitary condition of the army, and the efficiency of the hospitals. Its stores are always at the command of a judicious chaplain, who has an opportunity of properly distributing them. And every chaplain learns by experience, that a proper regard for the temporal wants of the men, and a reasonable effort on his part to relieve the needy, will always secure their sympathy and confidence, and will so predispose them in his favor, as greatly to aid him in instructing their minds in spiritual things, and winning them to Christ. And the more comfortable the sick and wounded are, as it respects quarters, bedding, food, and raiment, the more likely they are to listen attentively to the exhortations of the chaplain, in regard to the interests of the soul, and its eternal salvation.

The Christian Commission undertakes to provide not only for the temporal wants of the soldier, but to minister to his spiritual necessities; and nobly has it executed its mission, as far as its means have permitted it to prosecute its work. It goes forth into the camp and the hospital, with delicacies in one hand, the Bible in the other, and the voice of the living minister between them, and so endeavors to meet every want of the soldier, and to mitigate all his sufferings. Its every effort is blessing; and it has ever strewn its pathway, along the dreary wastes of war, with jewels of far more value than the diamond or the ruby, and which will sparkle with increased lustre and beauty, in the crown of the Redeemer's rejoicing, throughout the eternal years of his reign.

Many a chaplain has had cause for profound gratitude for the valuable aid rendered him by the Commission. It has saved life by the timely distribution of its stores; it has prevented untold sufferings on the part of sick and wounded men; and its delegates have been the means, under God, of the hopeful conversion of many precious and immortal souls. Its importance cannot be over-estimated; and it challenges the support of every friend of the chaplain, of the soldier, of the country, and of Christianity.

Judicious letters, written by friends to the soldiers, will aid the chaplain in his work. Every soldier, however humble his position, or high his rank, is the centre of a circle of "loved ones at home;" and a letter from any of them is always received with delight. There is a magic power in a tender and affectionate letter, which moves the stoutest heart, and moistens the fiercest eye. Let every letter to the soldier, from his beloved friends and relatives, burn with a pure and enlightened patriotism, and show a willingness to bear any sacrifice which the cause may demand; and it will fire his soul with a renewed determination to acquit himself like a man, and to press forward to deeds of still more noble daring. Let it speak of the love of Christ, and the freeness and fulness of the offer of salvation through his name, and of his power and willingness to save. Let it remind him of his covenant relations, his baptismal vows, and their solemn obligations. Let it assure him that he is daily remembered at the family altar, and urge him to pray on his own behalf. Let it kindly and affectionately remind him of the dangers of delay, in relation to a subject of such vital importance, and importune him, by every consideration of interest and love, to believe in the Lord Jesus Christ, and to enlist under his banner; and these truths and tender entreaties will move every heart, and cause many a careless soul to pause and reflect.

Every chaplain has seen the power of such letters in calling back the erring one to the path of duty, and in plucking others as brands from the burning, and, by the Spirit of God, securing their eternal salvation.

But, by the love which friends bear to their relatives in the army, let no unkind, morose, complaining letters be written by them. They annoy the soldier, dampen his spirits, sour his disposition, weaken his resolution, and are evil, and only evil. No good can ever come of them, either to the writer or the recipient.

The prayers of Christians assist the chaplain. It is an aid which can be given by all Christians, however rich or poor, however learned or illiterate. It is the least costly, but it is one of the most important and powerful means of aiding him, which is possessed by the friends of the soldier. It moves an arm which is almighty to deliver. It secures the blessings of the Holy Spirit, without whose gracious influences his labors will be in vain.

Many have been hopefully converted in the army, who have attributed their conversion to direct answers to the prayers of pious friends at home; and these conversions have often taken place under circumstances which have deeply impressed the mind of the chaplain with the same conviction.

There are many other ways, which will readily suggest themselves to their minds, by which the friends of the soldier may aid the chaplain; and he should be sustained by every means at their command. The moral and religious status of a million of men, who have been suddenly called from the peaceful pursuits of private life, and exposed to all the temptations of the camp, and all the perils of war, is a subject which challenges the most serious consideration of every Christian: but there are other issues involved in the matter, beyond the personal happiness of those actually engaged in arms.

A majority of these men will return to their families, and freely mingle in society; and as the defenders of the nation's honor, as the scarred warriors of many a bloody battle, as the heroes who have saved the life of the nation, and as the champions of liberty, they will wield a power which, for the present, will be irresistible. Their families will dote upon them; their friends will rejoice in them; young men and maidens will gather around them and listen to their thrilling narratives of dangers, privations, sufferings, and victories; and old men will do them honor. Surely no effort should be spared to thoroughly imbue their minds and hearts with the pure principles of Christianity, and to prevent them from becoming grossly immoral and vicious. On correct principles of political economy, no nation can afford to be indifferent to the moral and religious habits of so many of its prominent inhabitants. It involves the happiness of families, the peace of communities, and the ultimate safety of the State.

The chaplaincy is the great instrument by which the moral and religious forces of the Church are to be brought to bear upon the army. Without it, other agencies would do something, but their efforts would be occasional and fitful, and of little permanent advantage. Therefore, the practical issue is, either to sustain the chaplaincy, or to withdraw permanent religious services from the army. It is a channel, broad and deep, into which the streams of individual effort may empty, and form a majestic river, which shall flow through every valley and plain of the army, and bear upon its bosom blessings to every man; but which, separately, would for ever remain but the trickling mountain rivulet, at which occasionally a weary traveller might quench his thirst, and anon, a prowling wolf.

If its present organization is deficient, let its defects be ascertained and corrected. If the chaplain's duties are not sufficiently defined by law, let the law be amended. If he is subjected to unreasonable control of irreligious men, and his services liable to be interfered with by them, let him be disenthralled from such a position. If his legal status is anomalous and uninfluential, give him rank and official position, suited to his high character as a man, and the dignity of his ministerial office. If he is not held to sufficient accountability, give him a responsible head, and hold the department accountable for the efficiency of each of its members.

But let him be sustained. However much more might have been done, he has accomplished glorious things. The blessing of God has been upon his labors; and thousands of souls, who have been saved through his instrumentality, will ever chant the glorious song of redeeming love—"Unto him that loved us, and washed us from our sins in his own blood, and hath made us kings and priests unto God and his Father: to him be glory and dominion for ever and ever. Amen."

THE END.

www.ingramcontent.com/pod-product-compliance
Lightning Source LLC
Chambersburg PA
CBHW052053070526
44584CB00017B/2163